Single Moms Guide to Love and Money

Five Keys To Unlock Both

Dr. Lisa T. Lewis

All rights reserved. No part of this book may be used or reproduced in any manner whatsoever, including internet usage, without written permission from the author, except in the case of brief quotations embodied in critical articles and reviews.

ISBN 978-1-7355265-4-6

I dedicate this book to my two heartbeats:

Naomi Ruth and Frederick Duncan

Also, to my parents, Pastors James and Caroline Lewis for raising me so well, that I wanted to give all that love and more to my children, and your grandchildren.

To my family, all of yawl. If you just said, "she's talking about me", then you're right. Michael Todd. Nikki Bessie. Louis Andy. Juan Jose. Michael Dana. Althea. All of my cousins that are more like brothers, sisters, nieces, and nephews (Battle's, Lewis', Garnes', Green's). Aunts (Margaret, Vanjewell, Barbara, Marlene). Uncles (James, Joe, Thomas).

My Tribe: Danielle. Valisha. Canzada. Marcia. Rosalind. Terry. Rosa. Michelle. Tricia. Mary Ann. Katrina. The Smith Family. The Harris Family. The Taylor Family. The Owens Family. The Bobbitt Family. The Twyman Family. Sweet Liberty (Sandra, Jan, Regina, and Belina). Anointed Women In Christ (Chris, Latricia, Lynette, Tammy, and Harriett). Women Destined 4 Greatness. Women of Exchange.

I didn't want to start naming folks because I don't have enough room for everyone. If I mentioned this book to you and we are family or friends that are like family "My Tribe" includes you.

In Memoria:

Grandmother Mary. Grandmother Bessie. Grandaddy Lewis. Aunt Barbara Ann and Uncle David. Aunt Joyce. Uncle Bobby.

Contents

Welcome i
How To Use This Guide..ii

Guidepost I - Five Keys

Chapter 1
    Key #1: Faith... 1
Chapter 2
    Key #2: Fitness 5
Chapter 3
    Key #3: Finances 9
Chapter 4
    Key #4: Family and Friends 13
Chapter 5
    Key #5: Festivities 17

Guidepost II – LOVE

    Story – Leah... 21
Chapter 6
    Self-Love Makeover 23
Chapter 7
    Realizing Self-Worth 27
Chapter 8
    Becoming Self-Aware 31
Chapter 9
    Engaging in Self-Care 35
Chapter 10
    Acting With Self-Respect 39
Chapter 11
    Building Self-Esteem 43
Chapter 12
    Committing to Self-Growth... 51
Chapter 13
    Dating Tips for Single Moms..57
Chapter 14

Online Dating Made Simple 61
Chapter 15
    Summary – Self-Love Makeover 75

Guidepost III – MONEY

Story – Daughters of Zelophehad's 79
Chapter 16
    Not Just Money But Abundance 81
Chapter 17
    Financial Realty Therapy 85
Chapter 18
    What it Takes to Achieve a State of Financial Health 89
Chapter 19
    Negative Money Beliefs and Money Blocks 93
Chapter 20
    Positive Money Beliefs 97
Chapter 21
    How to Change a Belief 99
Chapter 22
    A Simple Plan of Action 107
Chapter 23
    Finding A Job In The New Economy 109
Chapter 24
    Tips To Negotiate Higher Starting Salary 127
Chapter 25
    Secondary Sources of Income 131
Chapter 26
    Summary: Money 135

Guidepost IV - Belief Systems

Story – Wisdom 139
Chapter 27
    No More Limits! Overcoming Your
    Self-Limiting Beliefs 141
Chapter 28
    Limiting Belief #1: I Don't Have Enough Time 143
Chapter 29
    Limiting Belief #2: I'm Too Old To
    Start Something New 149
Chapter 30
    Limiting Belief #3: Past Failure Means
    Future Failure 155
Chapter 31
    Limiting Belief #4: My Past Will Always
    Negatively Influence My Future 159

Chapter 32
    Limiting Belief #5: My Resources Are Limited 165
Chapter 33
    Limiting Belief #6: Lack Of Major Progress
    Means Failure 171
Chapter 34
    Limiting Belief #7: I Compare Myself To Others................ 177
Chapter 35
    Limiting Belief #8: I Am Not Responsible
    For My Current Situation 183
Chapter 36
    Limiting Belief #9: I Don't Deserve Success....................... 189
Chapter 37
    Limiting Belief #10: I Worry What
    Others Think About Me... 195
Chapter 38
    Limiting Belief #11: I Don't Give Myself
    The Love, Compassion, and Understanding
    I Give To Others...201
Chapter 39
    Limiting Belief #12: I Can Do Everything Myself...............207
Chapter 40
    Limiting Belief #13: I'm Not Smart Enough 213
Chapter 41
    Limiting Belief #14: I'm Not Ready To Start 219
Chapter 42
    Summary - No More Limits! Overcoming
    Your Self-Limiting Beliefs 225
Chapter 43
    Aha Moments 231
Chapter 44
    Transparency – My Why...233
About the Author..235

Welcome

I want you know that you are in a safe space. Single doesn't mean alone. Our time together is one of support, and encouragement.

Each chapter is set with the intention of sharing life-changing information to empower you to manifest and realize, your love and money goals.

Share this book with not only other single mothers but also with those that knows and loves a single mother.

Now turn the page to learn "How To Use This Guide" so you may get the most of our time together.

From my heart to yours,

Dr. Lisa

How To Use This Guide

Open your heart. Free your mind. Surrender to the flow.

This guide is intentionally and strategically organized.

I may create a companion journal in the future, but until I do so, have our journal and a pen available. There are exercises spread throughout the guide. Also, you may be inspired to act before you even finish reading. You want to be able to take notes and not have to worry about getting up and out of the "zone".

There are four guideposts: Keys, Love, Money, and Beliefs.

Each guidepost begins with a story. The story is a brief synopsis of a woman in the Bible that I believe encapsulates or demonstrates that guideposts.

Biblical women didn't have very many rights. They were property. Often to be seen and not heard. Relegated to being barefoot and in the kitchen. Servants and not many leaders.

However, each woman I highlight excels and succeeds, not despite but because of the times. Defying and changing the times, propelled them to greatness. So great, their stories are written in the Bible to be passed down from generation to generation.

Even if you aren't a Christian or don't believe the Bible is the Word of God, these women's stories are compelling, nonetheless.

If they can accomplish what they did in their day and time, what excuse do we have? Hint: NONE!

There story is at the beginning of each guidepost also to set the intention for the section.

There is one exception and that is found in the Guidepost IV – Beliefs section. I wanted to crush beliefs hard so there is a biblical woman's story highlighted by scripture at the start of each of those chapters. Again, to emphasize the possibility of overcoming a self-limiting belief and succeed in life. Allow the verse to minister to you.

Guidepost IV also includes Self-Reflection Questions to help facilitate a deeper experience eradicating that self-limiting belief.

Finally, at the end of each guidepost section is the "Summary". The summary includes:

- Practical Application – this section lists each of the keys and a suggestion on how to "apply". You are in now way limited to the one way I provide. Again, it's just pointing you in a direction. You are free and welcomed to go in whichever direction you feel inspired to go. Just going is the point.
- Prayer – a quick prayer to reveal, heal, and seal. Thanking God for revealing what we needed in that section. Asking God to heal the pain points that may arise. Finally, thanking God for sealing the deal and keeping His promises.

- Promise – aha! This section is all on you. While you were reading, what promises did you make to yourself? This is where you get to write those down. If it's not written, it's not real.

Guidepost I - Five Keys

"Take hold of my instructions; don't let them go.
Guard them, for they are the key to life".
Proverbs 4:13 (New Living Translation)

CHAPTER 1

Key #1: Faith

"Thus also faith by itself, if it does not have works, is dead." James 2:17 (New King James Version)

Exercising the Faith key is the lynchpin to unlocking the love and money goals outlined in this guide. This is not the pie-in-the-sky, sit back and wait for all this good stuff to come to you.

Faith as a key isn't a genie in a lamp either but an act of believing.

According to dictionary.com faith means, "confidence or trust in a person or thing".

I am a Christian. I have confidence and trust in God. I also have confidence and trust in myself. That confidence and trust isn't misplaced. In fact, I believe to have faith in God only and not in myself is a contradiction. Here why.

Christianity's foundation is that God created everything, including humankind. God created humankind in His image and likeness. God breathed into man, according to the scriptures, Genesis 2:7. We are the essence of God.

Our relationship to God is parallel to our relationship to our children. During the pregnancy phase, we nurture our children by how we care for ourselves. Remember the regular maternity doctor's appointments? I lost count of the number of times; my Gynecologist has to remind me that I was eating for two. I was resting for two. I was exercising for two. Everything I did, or ingested was impacting my unborn child.

I had faith that I had a child growing on the inside of me. The only way I was able to actually "see" them was on a sonogram screen. I felt them. I knew they were there. I believed they existed.

You see where I'm going now, right?

When my children were born and I saw them for the first time, what I had been working on for 38 weeks internally was now making its appearance in the flesh. I had confidence and trust that as long as I did what I could to properly provide for them, they would grow.

To believe in my children meant I had to believe in myself.

Faith.

Faith in the dictionary is a noun. Faith in conjunction with manifestation is a verb. Hence, the verse of scripture in James that mentions faith without works is dead. It's nonexistent.

Because we believe that we can achieve our love and money goals, we will do the corresponding work. That's why I can make the declaration with confidence to achieve any goal in life, we have to believe and do.

Examples:

Completing school requires going to class, doing the work, passing the tests to get promoted to the next grade.

Receiving a driver's license requires passing a test; written and driven.

Purchasing a home, if you don't pay cash, requires securing a mortgage. We secure mortgages by submitting all the paperwork to the bank and proving we are what? "trustworthy".

I could go on for the entire book.

As single mother, providing abundantly for our families, and still achieve our love and money goals, guilt-free and stress free will require the same faith and works.

Let's get to faithing!

CHAPTER 2

Key #2: Fitness

"But Jesus told him, "Anyone who puts a hand to the plow and then looks back is not fit for the Kingdom of God." Luke 9:62 (New Living Translation)

Am I ready to take on this challenge?

Do I have what it takes, time, energy, patience, mentally, emotionally, financially, etc.?

Typically, when we think of fitness, our minds automatically go to physical, right, and I'm going to get there, but that's not where we're going to start in terms of fitness. Where are we fitness-wise in terms of our mental health? We're going to talk about that. We're going to talk about our emotional health, our psychological health, and then last but not least, our physical health.

I am a cancer warrior. Part of my cancer has included getting genetic testing for other cancer risks. If you search "the Angelina Jolie Effect", you will get more information. Basically, a geneticist will test your DNA from saliva or a blood draw, for various cancer markers. If you test positive for a cancer or cancers, you work with your medical team to determine next steps.

Angelina Jolie, due to her mother's cancer history, took the cancer genetic test. She learned that genetically she had an 87% risk for breast cancer and 50% risk for ovarian cancer. This is public information she shared. As a result of the risk, she decided to have a double mastectomy and have both her ovaries and fallopian tubes removed. She reduced her risks down to single digits.

As of the writing of this book, I'm still awaiting my test results. I recorded my genetic counseling session and plan to record my result session as well. My goal is to not only share it with my family but also create a documentary to encourage more black women to get tested. Unfortunately, black women are more likely to die from breast cancer because they don't learn they have the disease until it's in the late stages.

I digress.

I will use my genetic testing experience to emphasis the importance of the fitness key to single mothers achieving their love and money goals.

First, we want to live long enough to raise our children into adulthood, see them get married, have our grandchildren. If we're lucky see some great-grandchildren as well. Alas, as of the writing of this book, I have no grandchildren. I do have a grand dog, Kenji.

Being a single mom takes much of what we have emotionally, psychologically, and physically. Just like the genetic counseling. You can't walk into your doctor's office and ask for a genetic test and get tested immediately without counseling.

Genetic counseling is required to do at least the following two things:

1. Geneticists – inform the patient of what to expect and possible impacts. She also determines if the patient is emotionally and psychologically able to handle the results. There is absolutely no coercion at ALL in this process.

    o At points in the discussion, I felt the opposite. I know that wasn't the case because she was trying to give me every possible scenario to help me make a fully informed decision about moving forward with testing.

    o After the counseling session, I had to sign paperwork that I was fully informed, aware, and accept the consequences and results of the test.

2. Patient – be honest with oneself and ask the hard questions. Am I ready to learn my genetic makeup? Am I ready to make the hard decisions if I learn I'm positive or have a risk for cancer or cancers?

    o How will my family be impacted by the news?

    o Can I wait the 2-3 weeks to get my results? I'm very impatient at times. The wait is HARD. Let me tell you.

    o How do I tell my children?

    o Am I emotionally, psychologically, and physically strong enough to walk this process through to the end?

The same applies to you moving forward in this guide and in achieving your love and money goals.

This is an informal love and money goal achievement coaching session. This guide you're reading is that.

Are you ready to receive the news that you have no more excuses? Are you ready to act and make the hard decisions? Yes. Yes, and yes again? Okay, let's talk finances next.

CHAPTER 3

Key #3: Finances

"Wisdom is even better when you have money. Both are a benefit as you go through life."
Ecclesiastes 7:11 (New Living Translation)

This may be the shortest chapter in the guide.

Living in general takes money. Raising children takes money.

According to spendmenot.com on average in the United States of America it costs $233,610.00 to raise a child until age 17. Need I say more?

Unless our child's father is from a wealthy family, chances are we will need to work to cover the majority of the $233K. Oh, and keep in mind that's the average.

Finances are so important in us attaining our goal to successfully raise our children, that is Guidepost II in this guide.

What's important to note her in regard to it being a key to achieving our love and money goals, is that it's okay to work for and want money.

I share my personal story of economic liberation in the TEDx Talk, "Progressing and pampering while parenting awakening to the possibility":

https://www.youtube.com/watch?v=jCpw8-xrah4

Having children is an investment of time and money. Investing in yourself first and then your children.

Yes, I know this feels and sounds counterintuitive, but I call it the Flight Attendant Principle. Before taking off on an aircraft the flight attendant gives the safety speech and demonstration. I'm paraphrasing:

"In the even of an emergency and we loose cabin pressure, the oxygen mask with release from the compartment above your head. Before helping anyone else, please securely place the oxygen mask on yourself first."

The Flight Attendant Principle means to me that I'm not even in a position to help anyone else until I help myself first. In the unfortunate attempt of me helping someone else first, I could die in the process. Consequently, not being very helpful at all.

Sit with that thought for a moment. Imagine that.

I apply that to my professional pursuits. I need to invest in myself and my career advancement to help and provide for my children. The power is in my hands. The power to get wealth is in your hands, Deuteronomy 8:18.

"Remember the Lord your God. He is the one who gives you power to be successful, in order to fulfill the cov-

enant, He confirmed to your ancestors with an oath." (New Living Translation)

Go get your money, Sis!

CHAPTER 4

Key #4: Family and Friends

"There is no greater love than to lay down one's life for one's friends." John 15:13 (New Living Translation)

Our children have us to support and encourage them. Who do we have? Family and friends.

Family doesn't have to be blood.

Dictionary.com

[10]"a group of people who are generally not blood relations but who share common attitude, interest, or goals and frequently live together"

Family is synonymous with tribe or group

Friend according to dictionary.com means, [1]"a person attached to another by feelings of affection or personal regard."

Friend is synonymous with ally, buddy, or partner

We need family. We need friends. I like to call them friends-like-family.

As single mothers, we are one another's tribe. We understand the challenges that we uniquely face being the primary custodian of our children. The buck stops with us.

It's healthy to need and ask for help.

I am a cancer warrior. I can't talk about my cancer journey with individuals that have never been personally challenged with cancer and expect them to understand. It is unfair and unreasonable of me to expect them to react as I would react because they aren't personally impacted.

How can I state this better?

As of the writing of this book both of my parents are still alive. Although as a clergywoman I have walked alongside individuals that have lost a parent or both parents, I don't "know" what they are feeling. I can imagine what they are feeling but I don't because both of my parents are still alive.

Yes, I sympathize but empathy comes from experience.

My Pastor, Pastor Sam, walked alongside me during my second cancer challenge. When he was speaking with me, he said something that brought tears to my eyes. He said, "Lisa, I don't know what you're going through. I haven't had your experience. But I can be here for you. I can hold a space for you to feel what you're feeling."

Wow. Pastor Sam's words were liberating. Unlike other well-meaning Christians that just told me to have faith. Believe God. Make positive confessions. Don't claim the report of the doctors.

I have faith but that doesn't make it any less devastating to learn about a cancer risk and diagnosis. I need family and friends-like-family to hold a safe space for me to feel what I'm feeling and be sympathetic.

Pastor Sam has been that. Other family and friends have been that as well.

As single mothers we need friends and family that are empathetic. Folks who know what it's like in the middle of the night to be thinking about what to do next to help our children. Praying and asking God for divine guidance on how to keep your children encouraged and healthy in every sense of the word.

Nothing takes God by surprise. God knew that we would be responsible for caring for these gifts, our children. God knows we have what it takes to raise them even when sometimes we feel like we are falling way short of the goal.

Having the support of other single mothers, family and friends makes the journey more palatable, and fun. I have lost count of the number of times my sister-friends offered childcare so I could get away for a weekend or just the day. Going to a non-G rated movie with not children in tow was a tremendous treat. I still enjoy going to the movies now my myself.

If you don't have a tribe, get one. Join my Single Moms Love and Money Facebook group. Join other Facebook groups with likeminded individuals.

Some churches in my area have Parents Without Partners. They are nationwide. Find a group near you. Heck, start one if you don't find one nearby.

According to the United Nations Women, 2020, there

are over 100 million single mothers globally. You're not in this alone. No woman is an island. Your tribe awaits.

CHAPTER 5

Key #5: Festivities

"The whole city celebrates when the godly succeed..." Proverbs 11:10 (The New Living Translation)

This may appear to be counterintuitive but throughout the Bible there are parties, festivals, celebrations.

- Celebrate Passover festival
- Celebrate three festivals
- Covenant feast to celebrate treaties
- Peace offerings—celebrate by feasting
- Festival of Unleavened Bread
- Annual festival
- Celebrate the Lords lovely name with music
- Celebrate when God speaks what is right
- Festival of the Harvest
- Celebrate with a feast when a child is weaned
- Leah named her son "Asher" which means "What joy is mine! Now the other women will celebrate with me."
- Celebrate the mighty acts of the Lord with music and singing
- Festival of Shelters

- New Moon Festival
- Sheep Shearers are at work...celebrate
- Prodigal son returned home...celebrate
- Celebrate peace
- Celebrate walls falling down
- Celebrate winning the war

These folks partied and ate for just about any reason at all. We need to do the same. Celebrate ALL wins; big or small.

It takes a lot of small wins to get to the big win anyway so why not enjoy the journey?

In the United States of America pennies are often disregarded. Because a penny is the smallest coin denomination that we have, you can find the on the ground. People will leave them in the tip jars in the local convenience store. One would think the penny didn't have any value.

My Budget Officer hat comes into play now. A nickel is five pennies. A dime is ten pennies. A quarter is twenty-five pennies. One dollar is sixty pennies. And so on. Pennies have value.

The small wins are just as valuable.

Failures are as valuable. Each failure is one step closer to success. Now that we know what doesn't work, we can try something new.

- Celebrate opportunities vailed as failure
- Celebrate open doors
- Celebrate closed doors – maybe when didn't need to go in that direction anyway

- Celebrate challenges – the experience shows us what we're made of—grit
- Celebrate applying for the job
- Celebrate getting an interview
- Celebrate unemployment – this is an opportunity to get refocused. Wait until you learn more in Guidepost III – Money
- Celebrate every birthday because everyone year is a milestone (thank you COVID)
- Celebrate faith
- Celebrate family and friends
- Celebrate fitness
- Celebrate your children
- Celebrate your life
- Celebrate Y-O-U

The same way we encourage our children to be successful at their chores, schoolwork, sports, life, etc. is the same way we need to encourage ourselves.

I remember sitting at my children's events; sports and plays and cheering for them so loudly from the sidelines. There were occasions that my children would ask me in advance of the event, not to be so loud. I was embarrassing them.

I had to explain to them how proud I was of them and their efforts. I wanted them to know that I was them for them. I wanted others to know that my kid is awesome, loved, and AMAZING. My kids appreciated the thought but still wanted me to pipe down. Laughing out loud.

It's highly likely you do the exact same thing.

We need to do the same for ourselves. Yes, even if that

means looking in the mirror and cheering for the person we see. Maybe that means while cooking dinner, we take a dance break. Can you tell I love to dance?

Whatever needs to happen that denotes celebration to you, do that. You don't need anyone's person. You don't even need anyone to celebrate with you. You are enough.

Party of one over here.

Who has the party hats, noisemakers, and cake?!

Guidepost II – LOVE

Story – Leah

Genesis 29:17-35
³²"When the Lord saw that Leah was unloved, He enabled her to have children..." (New Living Translation)

During my ministerial training, the trickery of Laban towards Jacob was discussed in depth. Even Rachel's story is told with vigor. However, Leah is often overlooked or glazed over.

I have always embraced Leah as an example of what life looks like when one learns to love themselves.

She wasn't Jacob's choice. In fact, the scriptures mention that Leah had no sparkle in her eye, but Rachel was beautiful. So not only wasn't she loved but she wasn't attractive either.

Leah's self-love in the beginning was so low that she names each of her sons in line with how she felt about herself and her God at the time of their births. It wasn't until she began to love herself, she had her fourth son and last child, Judah.

Judah means, "Now I will Praise the Lord". When she learned to love herself, she stopped having children (v35).

Leah birthed four of the twelve tribes. Through her womb came Jesus, the great High Priest, via Levi. Praise was birthed through Judah.

Who and what divine destiny have you been blessed to birth?

CHAPTER 6

Self-Love Makeover

How do you feel about yourself?

Would you say that you love yourself?

Don't take any more time to think about it – just answer now. You don't have to scream it out – especially if you are in public – but think of an answer right away.

OK, now that you have your answer in your head, let's engage in a couple of follow-up questions.

- Do you treat yourself with self-respect?
- Do you honor your personal preferences and make sure you address your self-care?
- You know how much you love that celebrity or Influencer. Do you love yourself that much?
- You know how you treat your best friends. Do you treat yourself like that?
- You know the people you'd do anything to help. Would you do the same for yourself?

Even if you originally answered that you loved yourself, I bet you started to question that decision when reading the follow-up questions. Many people will instinctively answer, "of course I love myself!" but then they start to wonder when they really think about it.

They question if they would ever treat a loved one like they treat themselves.

They wonder if they would ever talk to their loved ones like they talk to themselves.

Self-Love is about accepting and loving yourself for who you are while at the same time making sure your actions and behaviors follow suit.

It's hard to *truly* love yourself when:

- You are your own worst critic
- You judge yourself harder than you judge others
- You engage in destructive habits and behaviors
- You doubt your abilities
- You question your worth
- You engage in negative self-talk

If any of these behaviors sound familiar, then you might not love yourself as much as you think. And that's OK...

That is why you are here.

You are ready to experience a *Self-Love Makeover*. While you read this book, you get to be selfish. You are allowed to focus on yourself. You have permission to truly embrace who you are and fall in love with that person all over again.

The following pages of this book will focus on six different aspects of "the self":

- Self-Worth

- Self-Awareness
- Self-Care
- Self-Respect
- Self-Esteem
- Self-Growth

By committing to these six aspects, attitudes, characteristics, or whatever you want to call them, you will experience a Self-Love Makeover.

"Why Do I Care, Though?"

Fair question.

I know you shouldn't ask a question in response to a question, but I must – why wouldn't you?

Why wouldn't you care about self-love? Self-love isn't some weird new-age concept. It is common sense. Self-love is important because it is the bedrock of who you are as a person. If you can't accept and love yourself, you will be plagued with doubt your entire life.

The world is hard enough without being your enemy. Accepting who you are – warts and all - is an invaluable tool to help you move forward.

When you are committed to self-love:

- You will have less doubt and fear
- Your relationships will be more fulfilling
- You will be less anxious
- You will feel more satisfied and fulfilled in life
- You will see more opportunities
- You will be more capable of loving others

- You will achieve more and become more productive
- You will be able to assess your abilities honestly
- You will be healthier
- You will make healthier decisions
- You will be more comfortable in your own skin
- You won't tolerate being mistreated
- You will recognize your true worth
- You will be more empathetic towards others
- You will find your passions easier
- You will trust yourself more

This list could be another three pages long because the truth is – self-love will help improve *every area* of your life.

Are you sold yet?

Are you ready to admit that maybe you don't love yourself as much as you think, and it is time for a Self-Love Makeover?

If so, don't hesitate – it's time to jump right in and take the first steps towards a life where you truly love yourself. You will be surprised how much easier it is to tackle life's issues when you do so from a foundation of self-love.

CHAPTER 7

Realizing Self-Worth

There is zero hyperbole when I say this – if you learn this lesson, you could slam this book tight, never open it again, and it would still be worth 100x what you paid for it.

Self-worth is a simple concept. It is often confused or conflated with self-esteem, but the two concepts are quite different (more on self-esteem later). While self-esteem is an assessment of how you feel about yourself, self-worth is recognizing that you are still a valuable person worthy of love no matter how you feel.

Self-Worth is the most fundamental concept when it comes to self-love. You can't truly love yourself until you *accept that you are worthy of love in the first place.*

Nothing else we teach you will matter much at all if you can't accept that you are worthy of love. This is the first step to achieving almost any significant personal breakthrough.

Self-Worth & You

Do you feel like you are a good person who deserves to be treated with love and respect? If you don't, you need to work on that before you move on in this book.

The problem is, there isn't really a one-size-fits-all solution to develop your self-worth, either. We can't tell you exactly how to accept who you are since every person will face their own personal issues.

People's self-worth could be lagging due to any number of problems that we can't possibly predict with any accuracy.

However, we can still help you avoid some of the common traps that people searching for self-worth fall into. Even more important than knowing what our self-worth is tied to is knowing what it is not tied to.

Your self-worth is never defined by:

- How you compare to others
- What you have (or haven't) achieved
- Your career
- Societal expectations
- Social media "likes"
- What other people think about you
- Your weaknesses (or strengths)
- The size of your friend list
- How much you earn
- Anything or anyone except yourself

It's time to let go of the above list and finally believe in your self-worth. Say it out loud with me:

I am worthy of love and respect.

Say it again!

I am worthy of love and respect.

One more time for the people in the nosebleeds…

I am worthy of love and respect.

Seven words, simple but powerful. It might help if you regularly repeat these words like an affirmation. Maybe it helps if you write it down and keep it somewhere in sight.

Regardless of your methods, drill that message into your head until you truly believe it. No matter who you are, you deserve love. You are worthy of it. You are a human being who has value and importance.

If you are struggling with accepting your self-worth, you might want to consider speaking with a professional. If you don't have the means or don't think it has reached that point – then talk to a loved one.

Remember, this lesson is the crux of the entire Self-Love Makeover. If you can't find a way to feel worthy, you will never love yourself.

CHAPTER 8

Becoming Self-Aware

The next concept you need to think about is self-awareness.

Self-awareness is the ability to see and understand yourself clearly and objectively.

The funny thing is you might be surprised by your wants and desires.

We all think we know what we want and who we are, but it isn't until we intentionally reflect on it that we truly learn.

Self-awareness is an important aspect of your self-love makeover. It is a vital step in the journey towards self-love because knowing yourself is the first step to loving yourself.

How can you love yourself if you don't even know "who" you are?

Being aware of what you want and what you are capable (or not) of is also important in general terms. Never mind The Self-Love Makeover. How can you have any direction in life when you don't know what you want or value?

Self-awareness includes knowledge of:

- Your desires
- Your values
- Your strengths
- Your weaknesses
- Your habits
- Your traits
- Your feelings
- Etc.

Remember, people, change as well. Practicing self-awareness means *regularly* checking in with yourself so you know what's going on.

One of the best ways to accomplish this is to start journaling. Journaling offers many health and wellness benefits, so it is a good habit to start, no matter your reason.

Often, people struggle with journaling because they don't know what to write. Since your goal is to build self-awareness, this shouldn't be a problem for you. If you are struggling, though, here are some journal prompts you should work through.

Note: You can answer all these questions in a single journal post or make a journal post for each question. The goal is to eventually work through each question before moving on in this book, though.

20 Self-Awareness Prompts

1. What do I want out of life?
2. What are my core values?

3. What are my strengths?
4. What are my weaknesses?
5. What gives my energy?
6. What saps my energy?
7. What can't I live without?
8. What do I need to be happy?
9. How do I deal with negative thoughts or feelings?
10. When am I most productive?
11. What are my biggest distractions?
12. What is my biggest fear?
13. What is my definition of happiness?
14. What would a normal day look like in my ideal world?
15. What kind of person do I want to be?
16. What is working well in my life?
17. What isn't working well in my life?
18. What would I change in my life with the wave of a magic wand?
19. What accomplishments make me feel proud?
20. What motivates me?

Answering these 20 questions is a strong start towards self-awareness. Don't feel limited by this list, though. Feel free to add and answer your own questions, as long as they are reflective and introspective about who you are as a person.

You also probably noticed that not every one of these questions is positive. That is fine! Remember our self-worth lesson? You need to find yourself worthy and valuables despite any issues you have. The Self-Love Makeover isn't about ignoring your faults. It's about recognizing them, accepting them, and then taking the required steps to address them.

Note: We suggested journaling as a self-awareness technique because it is something you can do regularly. The answers to these questions may change over time, so don't shy away from answering the same questions repeatedly. Comparing your current answers to past answers will offer even more insight into yourself.

CHAPTER 9

Engaging in Self-Care

The third aspect of the Self-Love Makeover is self-care.

Self-Care is exactly what it sounds like - caring for yourself and your needs. More importantly, though, self-care is not:

- Selfish
- Greedy
- Indulgent

We must make this clear because so many of you struggle with this idea. Many people are so caught up caring about their partner, children, family, friends, and colleagues that they find the thought of self-care to be indulgent.

This feeling of indulgence could not be further from the truth!

Self-care is vital – especially currently. People find it harder to unwind and slow down. If you don't care for your needs, you can suffer serious consequences like burnout, depression, or anxiety.

Note: *if you feel like you suffer from the issues mentioned above, please reach out to a trusted loved one.*

If you are still struggling to see the importance of self-care, consider this. You want to help and care for the people in your life, right? You might care so much about it that you let your self-care slide.

This is an issue.

Have you ever flown on a commercial flight? The flight attendant will tell you that if things go wrong and the airplane is depressurized, oxygen masks will drop. They stress the importance of putting your mask on first before you help others. After all, if you can't breathe, you won't be able to help the people around you. Instead of being helpful, you will soon find that you are the one in need of help.

You can similarly think of self-care.

While it is great that you want to help the people in your life, it will eventually catch up to you if it means you ignore your care.

Self-care is vital to the Self-Love Makeover. If you want to love yourself truly, you need to prove it by treating yourself with care.

Self-Care Checklist

Here are some different areas of your life that you should introduce self-care.

Physical

- Are you eating well?
- Do you get enough exercise?
- Do you feel in control of your health?

- How are you sleeping?

Mental

- Do you have an outlet for stress?
- Have you considered unplugging from social media?
- Do you have hobbies or pursuits that allow you to relax?
- Have you discussed your mental well-being with loved ones?

Social

- Are you seeing your friends enough?
- Do you have healthy, fulfilling relationships?
- What do you need to feel more socially satiated?
- How do you nurture your important relationships?
- Do your friends and family know your needs?

Spiritual

- Do you feel spiritually fulfilled?
- Are your comfortable talking about your spirituality?
- Do you engage in any spiritual practices?
- Do you regularly reflect on how your spirituality affects your life?

Emotional

- Do you have healthy ways to process your emotions?
- Do you have people you can talk to about your emotions?
- How do you manage extreme emotions?

- Do you practice any mindfulness techniques like meditation?

Remember, self-care isn't a luxury. It is vital to your happiness, fulfillment, and yes – even productivity.

You can't love yourself if you aren't willing to care for yourself.

CHAPTER 10

Acting With Self-Respect

Can you love yourself if you don't respect yourself?

Self-respect is the next important aspect of the Self-Love Makeover. It is like self-worth, in that you need to recognize your worth, but different because it demands certain actions and behaviors.

For this guide, consider self-*worth* as feeling like you are worthy of respect, while self-*respect* is how you act to honor that feeling.

Acting with self-respect is so important because, without it, you open yourself up to all sorts of bad behavior from others:

- Demands on your time
- Being used
- Your wishes not being respected
- General mistreatment

Worse yet, when you don't act with self-respect, you become a target for troubled individuals like narcissists. These narcissists, and other unsavory characters, prey on people they can control.

How Can I Act with Self-Respect?

Acting with self-respect isn't that hard. You should just treat yourself how you'd treat people you already respect. You don't demand and expect other people to give up their autonomy and do whatever you want, so why should they get to dictate the same to you?

Set Better Boundaries

You get to control how you spend your time. If someone asks you to do something that isn't your responsibility – let that person know about it. If someone is infringing on your time too much, let them know you need a break.

Remember, "no" is a full sentence. If you tell someone no, or set a boundary with someone, you don't need to explain why. If this person can't deal with that, then it is their problem.

Don't Allow People to Mistreat You

People who respect themselves don't allow others to talk down to them or treat them poorly. You are worthy of respect and if someone habitually steps over the line with you – let them know it's not OK.

This conflict can be hard if it is a close loved one or someone with power in your life (like your boss), but no one should get a pass to mistreat you.

Avoid Toxic People

You are worthy of dependable, reliable, and uplifting relationships. If you have someone in your life who just saps your energy, brings you down, or otherwise isn't a good friend – consider moving on from them. If you can't drop them or avoid them entirely, consider figuring out ways to limit their access to you as much as possible.

Say No More Often

I often say, "No is my ministry".

It's not always easy to tell someone "No," but you should get used to it. If someone asks you to do something you don't have the time or means to accomplish, it is better to say no than pretend like you can handle it.

Likewise, suppose someone is infringing on your time by asking you to do something that isn't your responsibility. In that case, it is fine to say no. Helping people out is a wonderful trait but be careful people don't try and take advantage of you.

Stick to Your Core Values

Remember back in the self-awareness section when you defined your core values?

Don't be swayed to go against the things you truly believe in just for social acceptance. You are worthy of having your own beliefs, and people should respect that. If one of your beliefs happens to conflict with societal expectations, who cares? As long as you aren't hurting other people, you are entitled to act upon your own beliefs and values.

Don't Hide Your Emotions

Your emotions are as valid as anyone else's. Don't feel like you need to hide your emotions to make other people feel comfortable. In fact, bottling up your emotions is an unhealthy habit that can have long-term mental and physical effects.

Don't Rely on Others for Fulfillment

Much too often, you sacrifice your own needs and beliefs to make other people in your life happy. Subconsciously, you are scared of losing these people because your self-respect is tied to their feelings about you. No one should have that control over you.

Of course, everyone does things for and makes compromises with people they love. This altruism is natural and healthy. However, if your whole sense of worth is tied to your relationship, you don't respect your value.

Self-respect is vital to your Self-Love Makeover. Acting with self-respect will make loving yourself that much easier. It isn't hard either. Follow the above steps, and if you need more guidance, consider this:

Figure out how you would treat the people you respect the most. This is how you deserve to be treated.

CHAPTER 11

Building Self-Esteem

We mentioned self-esteem earlier when we described the nuance between self-esteem and self-worth.

Self-esteem is how you view yourself.

It's the subjective sense of your skills and abilities. Essentially, it's how capable you feel. When you feel confident you can accomplish something, that is your self-esteem talking.

It doesn't take much imagination to figure out how self-esteem is tied to the Self-Love Makeover. Ask yourself this; Can you truly love yourself if you doubt your ability to ever accomplish anything?

Is It Really That Important?

It is crucial, especially when you consider its importance to self-love.

When you think about it, healthy self-esteem boosts all the other aspects of the Self-Love Makeover.

- It makes it easier for you to feel self-worth.

- You will be more confident about your wants and needs when you consider your self-awareness.
- It will be much easier to set boundaries and say "no" to honor your self-respect.
- You will feel like you truly earned that bit of respite self-care provides.
- Committing to self-growth (more on this later) will feel like a natural extension.

Self-esteem is also important completely on its own. It will impact every decision you make and every action you take. A healthy self-esteem can help you:

- Make quicker/better decisions
- Boost mental health
- Handle adversity better
- Cope with stress
- Set and reach big goals
- Feel more fulfilled and satisfied
- Be more assertive
- Act more confidently
- And of course, *love* yourself

And that last point is why we are here, after all – to love ourselves!

Time for another quick self-assessment: *How do you think your self-esteem measures up. Do you feel generally confident about your abilities? Do you think overall you are a capable person?*

If you find this question difficult to answer, consider the following signs. If you exhibit any combination of these behaviors, your self-esteem may be lacking.

Signs You Might Lack Self-Esteem

- You define yourself by past mistakes and failures
- You feel like you are lacking control in your life
- You don't like to ask for things even when you need them
- You don't stand up for yourself
- You take criticism too personally
- You are a people-pleaser
- You don't feel needed
- You engage in negative self-talk
- You don't take risks
- New opportunities seem too daunting
- You apologize even when there is no need
- You shy away from contributing during discussions
- Even the simplest decisions flummox you
- You have a negative outlook about life in general
- You struggle with compliments

If you can relate to several of these, you are likely struggling with your self-esteem.

If you do struggle with self-esteem issues, it is important to face them head-on. No one's self-esteem ever got better by just sitting around and wallowing in it. You need to come up with a plan to boost your self-esteem and then tackle it.

The funny thing is, simply creating the plan to tackle your self-esteem is likely to boost it. Just imagine what successfully acting on the plan could do!

To help you out, we have included a seven-step process that will help you start boosting your self-esteem.

Seven Steps to Save Your Self-Esteem

1. Identify Your Negative Beliefs

The first step to dealing with your self-esteem issues is identifying the negative beliefs you have about yourself. Reflect on how you think about yourself. What negative self-talk do you engage in regularly?

Quite often, your thoughts or self-talk will begin with phrases like:

- I can't...
- I'll never be able to...
- I'm not good enough to...
- I don't have any...
- Etc.

Any time you catch yourself thinking or talking to yourself like this, jot it down.

Note: *Remember the journal we mentioned earlier? This step is another perfect opportunity to use it.*

2. Challenge Your Negative Beliefs

Once you have brainstormed a list of all your negative thoughts and self-talk, write down some reasons why they aren't true. Think about any evidence you have that would make your negative belief seem silly.

For example:

If you wrote "I'm just not good at making friends," challenge that by writing down the traits you have that would make a good friend.

If you wrote, "I don't have the skills I need to move up the ladder at work," challenge that by writing down the skills you do have or brainstorming ways you could acquire the needed skills.

Make sure you come up with evidence that challenges all your negative beliefs. The evidence is there, no matter how hard it is for you to see it.

3. Identify Your Strengths and Abilities

You may have already done this step in the self-awareness section. If so, refer to that list. If not, take the time now to list your:

- Strengths
- Personal abilities (i.e., good communication)
- Physical abilities (i.e., strong)
- Your interests

4. Set Goals That Honor Your Strengths and Abilities

Setting goals is a powerful way to boost your self-esteem. People who have goals – especially those written down – are more likely to show signs of healthy self-esteem.

One of the best ways to boost your self-esteem is to set goals that honor your current abilities and interests. You will find the goals easier to achieve, and you will be more motivated to accomplish them.

Not all your goals need to reflect your skills and interests but having one or two can help keep your self-esteem level.

Here is a quick example. If you are skilled in wilderness survival, you love camping, and your strengths are stamina and fitness – create a goal to finish a multi-day hike through wild terrain.

5. Make a Plan

Once you have a goal or two, plan on how to achieve it. List every step you need to take to achieve your goal.

Each step of your plan will become a new micro-goal. Don't think any step is too small to list – this will become important when it comes to taking action.

The act of creating a plan to achieve a goal is very empowering. It is likely to boost your self-esteem all on its own.

6. Act Quickly

Remember we said that no step in your plan is too small? That was important because you need to act quickly. Once you have your plan, act on the smallest, most simple step.

For example, if you wanted to do a multi-day hike, one of your micro-goals might be researching where to go. If that is the case, find and research three spots that you could realistically accomplish this goal. Do it right away.

The sense of accomplishment you feel upon finishing a step of your plan is the single best way to boost your self-esteem. The more steps you accomplish, the better you will feel.

7. Reflect & Repeat

Once through this list isn't going to sustain your self-esteem. The idea here is to repeat this goal setting and planning whenever you reach (or abandon) one of your existing goals.

When you finish (or abandon) a goal from above, reflect on it. How did it make you feel? What did you learn about yourself? What did you learn that can help you with future goals? What mistakes did you make? Did you learn from them?

Bonus Step: Affirm Your Worth in The Face of Failure

We mentioned abandoning your goal above. Please don't view that as purely negative. Sometimes circumstances and goals change. It is fine! If a goal no longer serves your needs or reflects your values, it is OK to move on.

Even if you have failed along the way – don't let this get you down. You can flip failure into a self-esteem-boosting lesson.

The next time you are dealing with a failure, make a list of your related qualities. For example, if you don't get the promotion you wanted, make a list of the reasons you deserved it. If you took a shot and asked out a crush, just for them to say no, write down reasons you'd make a quality partner.

Now, please choose a quality from the list above. Expand on it with a few paragraphs about why people should value the quality. Explain why people will likely appreciate the quality in the future.

CHAPTER 12

Committing to Self-Growth

Self-growth is the final aspect of the Self-Love Makeover, but don't let the late inclusion make you doubt its importance. A commitment to self-growth is one of the most important ways you can show love to yourself.

Self-growth is a commitment to learning and growing as a person. You may have heard the terms *personal growth* or *personal development* used instead. For our purposes, you can use the terms interchangeably.

Self-growth is the process of improving yourself by your actions.

Once your school days are over, some people are ready to cruise. Sure, your job might train you on a specific skill, but that isn't really *your* action now, is it? The skill might be so niche that it doesn't help you out in any other area of your life.

Ignoring self-growth is how many people become stuck or stagnant. Can you love yourself if you are content with stagnation? The world is rushing around you like a river while you try to stay still. How long before the water knocks you down, or worse yet, drags you under?

Practicing self-love draws you naturally towards self-growth. You want the best for yourself, and a commitment to learning and growth is part of that!

Some examples of self-growth include:

- Learning to control your emotions
- Learning a new skill
- Learning a new language
- Engaging in a new hobby
- Breaking bad habits
- Developing good habits
- Becoming more responsible
- Changing or adjusting your mindset
- Becoming more empathetic
- Perfecting an art or pursuit
- Becoming a (better) leader
- Building resilience
- Better stress management.

The Importance of Self-Growth

Even if you ignore the Self-Love Makeover aspect, a commitment to self-growth is a healthy and intelligent choice. Just look at the list above, do any of those examples seem like a bad idea? Not really. They all look like wonderful ways to enrich your life.

Enriching your life is a great way to show that you love yourself. On top of enriching your life (maybe in addition to), self-growth can impact your life in many positive ways:

- Avoid boredom
- Avoid getting stuck in the past

- Continually improve your results
- Stay engaged
- Stay relevant
- Keep a sharp mind
- Feel younger
- Boost your memory
- Feel happier and more fulfilled
- Get ahead in your career and life
- Grow emotionally

This list is hardly exhaustive. To put it briefly – committing to self-growth is one of the best ways you can positively impact your life.

So, How Do I Commit to Self-Growth?

So, are you sold on the power of self-growth? Congrats! You have already taken the first step.

Step 1: Recognize

The first step towards committing to self-growth is to recognize its importance. You need to accept that change is inevitable, and if you don't continue to grow, you will be left behind.

Step 2: Needs

What skills or abilities do you need to move forward in life? Think about what you need to learn to progress in your career and life.

Make sure you consider tangible skills you might need. For example, the only way to progress at your current job may include learning a new programming language. This is a tangible skill that you can acquire – usually through schooling or training.

Don't forget the less tangible skills as well. For example, the programming training is great, but you will need to manage a team if you get this promotion. Maybe that means you need to learn how to control your emotions a bit better. You might need to become more positive to set an example for your team. This kind of growth will include more personal reflection rather than classroom training.

Actionable Step: Brainstorm a list of tangible and intangible skills that could help you progress in any area of your life.

Step 3: Desires

Not all your self-growth will be skills, attributes, or traits that you *need* per se.

You might have a desire for growth just for the sake of your personal preferences. Learning a new instrument might not help you pay the bills, but it could help you feel happier and more fulfilled.

Likewise, you might want to brush up on an old hobby just for fun. You might want to join a class more for social interaction. It doesn't matter what the goal of your self-growth is, just as long as you keep growing.

This is the Self-Love Makeover, after all. Doing something solely because it makes you happy isn't just acceptable – it is encouraged!

Actionable Step: Brainstorm a list of things you'd like to learn just for sheer enjoyment.

Step 4: Focus

Self-growth is a process. It isn't something that happens overnight, so don't force it. Now that you have a couple of different lists of ways you'd like to grow, learn and evolve, it is time to pick one (or maybe two) thing(s) to focus on first.

Focus is very important. Learning and growing can be intense, so learning too many things at once will likely lead to failure. Plus, would you like to learn one or two things impeccably or have nothing but a passing knowledge of several different topics?

You have your entire life to grow and evolve, so there is no need to rush. Once you are comfortable with your growth in one area, you can move on to another.

Actionable Step: Choose one topic or skill to learn.

Step 5: Plan

You already know what time it is! It is time for you to plan how you will learn whatever topic you choose from above.

This topic will likely fall into two categories: self-taught or instruction from someone else. If you are going the self-taught method, your plan will need to be more detailed.

- How are you going to achieve this growth?
- What do you need to achieve this?
- How long should it take to achieve this growth?
- Can anyone help me achieve this?

Treat your chosen area of growth as a goal. Break it down

into as small as steps as possible. Just like you learned in the last section, this will make taking action easier when it is time.

Actionable Step: Choose the simplest step and take it.

Step 6 - Commit

You have a plan for self-growth, so the only thing you need to do now is commit to it.

Figure out a way to incorporate this growth into your daily routine. If daily is too much, work on it weekly. When it comes to life-long growth, it's more important to be consistent in the long-term than productive in the short.

Actionable Step: A great way to help your commitment is to schedule a time to work on your self-growth pursuits. Take a few minutes now to block off some time in your calendar to work on your new pursuit.

Self-growth is one of the surest ways you can love yourself. It shows a commitment to your mental and physical well-being. At the same time, self-growth will propel you forward, ensuring that you don't get left behind.

The question isn't, "Is Self-Growth important?" The real question is do you love yourself enough to commit to it.

CHAPTER 13

Dating Tips for Single Moms

If you're single and have children, dating can be somewhat challenging. However, **it's possible to be a great parent and still enjoy taking part in dating** and developing close relationships with other adults.

Try these dating tips for single moms:

1. Vow to keep your parenting life and your dating life separate until appropriate. Consider your dating life as an activity you do the occasional evening as an adult social activity.

2. Strive to achieve a certain balance in your life. Ensure that how you spend your time on a day-to-day basis demonstrates your life's priorities.

3. Avoid involving your children with everyone you date. One of the most difficult things for a child after his parents separate is being exposed too soon to a parent's "new" partner.

    o *Protect your kids from uncomfortable feelings by not involving them with your dates.*

    o Recognize that, even if you really like someone you've gone out with 2 or 3 times, you don't know for sure at that point that the relationship will "work out" and become long-term. If you involve your child and it doesn't work out, your child is again placed in the vulnerable position of feeling rejected, left behind and hurt.

4. Set limits regarding dating and parenting efforts with your children. Be upfront and honest about how much time you'll spend with someone you date.

    o For example, if you feel you can't be out past a certain time or can't go out two nights in a row because of your parenting duties, be open about it. *Doing so shows you're clear and confident about what's important to you.*

5. Share your feelings with the person you're dating. If you're disappointed, you're unable to spend more time with the person you're dating, tell them.

    o This way, they'll know what you're going through and hopefully grow to understand your position as a parent who's striving to have a healthy social life.

6. Let your kids know that they're your first priority. Regardless of just telling them so, demonstrate through your behavior that you love your kids and are interested in all their activities.

    o Make a major effort to attend your kids' school functions and extracurricular activities, such as sports, dance and music recitals.

7. From time to time, talk with your children in gener-

al about your dating life. Tailor your talk based on the age of your children.

- o Explain that you like to have fun with other adults and that there will be times that you go out with friends.
- o Let them know a couple of days in advance that you'll be going out.

8. Your time out can be an opportunity to make life interesting and fun for your kids. For example, occasionally, let them stay over with Grandma and Grandpa when you have a date. Your kids most likely enjoy spending time with their grandparents.

- o Or find a teenager close by that you know and trust. Usually, kids love to have teenagers for babysitters.
- o *As long as you know the kids will be well cared for and safe, make the time they spend without you fun.*

You can truly enjoy this time of your life. Even though you're a parent, you can set aside time to date. Make an effort to balance your single-parenting life and your dating life. When you do, you'll discover the joys of both.

CHAPTER 14

Online Dating Made Simple

Online dating makes it easy to meet new people and find love.

However, dating online isn't the same as having your friends set you up. It requires a different approach.

You need a strategy to find success with online dating.

Your profile, messages, and photos are an important part of online dating. You'll also want to watch out for catfishing and other scams.

Discover how to navigate the waters of online dating with these top tips.

Start by Making Lists

The first step to finding success with online dating is to make several lists.

A good plan will save you time and effort while searching for a partner online. It's important to do the planning before trying to create a profile or upload a photo.

Consider making these lists:

1. Make a list of your goals. What do you want to accomplish with online dating?

    o Do you want to meet your soulmate, or are you looking for a casual relationship?

    o Figure out what you want to get out of online dating.

    o Write down what you're looking for in a potential partner.

2. Make a list of dating websites. Create a list of all the dating websites you plan to use and check them out first.

    o Take a look at each website and read the requirements.

3. Make a list of ideas for your profile. Write down everything you want to include. Then, narrow it down and only keep the most important points.

By making these lists, you'll be better prepared for a positive experience.

Online Dating Profile Tips

Your profile is an important part of online dating. It has to be accurate, fun, and attractive.

You want to share your personality and make it easy for people to connect with you.

Research shows that shorter profiles tend to do better

online. However, you want to ensure that you include enough information.

Try these ideas for your online dating profile:

1. Keep it short and interesting. Include enough information to pique their interest without being long or boring. There's no need to share every detail of your life.

2. Avoid common turn-offs. Bragging and lying are common issues that it's better to avoid.

    o Avoid exaggerating in your profile. People will notice you're bragging and won't connect.

    o Be original in your dating profile. Don't copy another profile or the content. Show the real you to the world.

    o Avoid sharing your baggage or issues. An online profile isn't the place to discuss childhood trauma. It's okay to discuss these topics later with a partner.

3. Create curiosity. Share just enough information to create curiosity.

4. Check spelling and grammar. It's important to check the grammar and spelling in your profile before publishing it. Many people are turned off by mistakes and think it's sloppy.

    o A tiny typo isn't an issue. However, multiple mistakes can make others think you don't care.

    o For some people, grammar and spelling errors are a pet peeve.

Your profile is one of the most important parts of finding love online. Use these tips to make it interesting and fun to read.

Photo Tips

Your photo is one of the first things people notice online. They may only spend a few minutes scanning the text, but they always pay attention to pictures.

Consider posting several recent photos on your profile.

You want people to see the real you, so avoid using filters or Photoshop.

Use these photo tips:

1. Use a recent photo. Add a recent photo to your online profile. Avoid choosing one that is old or unflattering.

    o No one wants an unpleasant surprise on a first date, so it's important to use a recent picture. People should be able to recognize you easily in it.

    o It's a good idea to include several recent photos.

2. Avoid using photos with friends. Although it's fine to post photos with friends on social media, you want to avoid doing this on your online profile. People want to see you and not a group of friends.

    o It's sometimes hard to figure out who is in group photos. This could confuse potential dates.

    o Group photos may also show a lack of confidence.

3. Avoid inappropriate photos. Some online dating sites will take down inappropriate photos and block the profiles.

    o You can send the wrong impression to potential dates.

    o Revealing photos can make you look desperate. They can also lead to inaccurate expectations on first dates.

4. Use photos that show activity. Do you have photos that show you hiking or traveling?

    o Activity photos can help potential dates get to know you better. They can show them a different side of your personality.

    o Consider using photos from trips or vacations.

5. Think about including pets. If pets are a big part of your life, consider including them in your photos. However, avoid putting pets in every single picture you post.

    o It's important to have a variety of pictures with pets and without them. Your dates may be interested in this.

6. Include at least one body shot. Some people skip profiles without any body shots.

    o A photo showing all of you that is fully clothed is a good addition to the profile. Some people get worried when the only photos they see are close-ups of your face.

- A body shot lets them know you have nothing to hide.
- It also shows that you have confidence in your looks.

Photos can make or break your online profile. Always use recent photos that reveal the real you.

Messaging Tips

Most online dating websites include the option to message potential dates.

You'll want to master this part of the dating world. Your messages can either convince someone to date you, or they can make them run away screaming.

Consider these messaging tips:

1. Reply within a reasonable time. Messaging on a dating website isn't the place to play hard to get.
    - Reply within a reasonable amount of time. Your potential date will move on if they don't get an answer. Making them wait won't make you more desirable.
    - Try to reply to messages within 24 hours unless you're traveling or extremely busy.
    - Be considerate of others, but you can skip replying to spam messages.
2. Have reasonable expectations. Give others a chance to respond to your message before getting angry.
    - Keep in mind that some people create dating profiles and don't check them every day.

- Wait for a response to your first message before sending more.
- Avoid expecting them to drop everything and message a stranger. They may have work, school or other obligations that keep them busy.
- Don't assume they aren't interested in you if you don't hear back right away.

3. Wait before messaging your number. Before sharing your personal phone number, exchange multiple messages on the dating website.

   - By getting to know someone in a safe, controlled environment, you're less likely to make mistakes. In addition, you're able to ask more questions.
   - Once someone has your phone number, it's harder to get rid of them.

4. Avoid giving out too much personal information. It's okay to talk about your work or hobbies with a potential date but be careful about what you share. Giving out too much personal information may be dangerous.

   - Avoid sharing your address, birthdate, or work location until you really know the other person.
   - Never share your social security number, banking information, or credit cards with strangers on dating sites. They may be scammers trying to steal your information.
   - Never post your driver's license or birth certificate online.

- Your personal information needs to stay private. You shouldn't feel pressured to share it.

5. Watch your language. Emoticons and slang are normal parts of messaging but avoid cursing.

    - Keep your language casual and warm without being presumptuous.
    - Avoid cursing or other things that can make a potential date uncomfortable.

6. Remember that texts aren't love. It's easy to get lost in the text messages on an online dating website. However, they're just one small part of a relationship.

    - Some people send messages without wanting a serious relationship.
    - Loving texts don't always translate into love in the real world.
    - Keep in mind that some people find it easier to text than to talk on a phone or in person.

Messaging another person on an online dating site can help you get to know them. Take advantage of this feature to get to know someone before meeting them in person.

Avoid Catfishing and Other Dangers

Online dating can be a fun way to meet new people and potential love interests, but it has a dangerous side.

There are many dangers in the online dating world that can put you at risk. From scammers who want to steal your personal information to catfishers who lie about their identity, you really never know who you're dealing with during your initial contacts. It's important to be careful.

For your own safety, keep these tips in mind:

1. Understand catfishing. Catfishing means luring another person into a relationship by using a fake identity online.

   o Catfishing is one of the most common issues with online dating.

   o Some people use fake photos and information to start relationships. They take these situations to extremes and will even set up dates.

   o There are many reasons why someone may use catfishing. For some, it's a game and a joke. For others, it's a twisted way to exploit people.

2. Always meet in public. Avoid meeting in private or secluded areas.

   o Always meet a potential date in a well-known public place with a lot of people.

   o Ensure your friends or family know where you'll meet the person.

   o Consider taking a trusted friend with you on your first date, so you're not alone.

3. Avoid falling for scams. There are many online dating scams that scammers use to get money out of strangers - or from YOU!

   o The scammers may pretend to have an emergency or a sick family member. They may ask for money to see a doctor or visit a friend. They may even pretend to have cancer.

- o Another common scam is to ask for money to come see you.
- o Some scammers pretend they don't have money but are madly in love with you. They may ask for money to buy a plane ticket or get a visa.
- o Refuse to send money to strangers, even if they claim to love you.

4. Always investigate. It's important to do some investigating before meeting a person you found online.

- o Do a search for their name and picture online.
- o Check out their social media accounts and websites. See who they're connected to online and what they post.

Remember these tips to stay safe, alert, and avoid the dangers that can lie in wait for you through online dating sites.

Online dating can certainly help you meet a potential partner.

For your best experience, create an interesting, true-to-life profile with recent pictures, learn to use messaging correctly, get to know potential dates before meeting in a public place, and be alert to dangers like scammers and catfishing.

Keep these tips in mind and enjoy your online dating

adventures! Who knows? You could meet the partner of your dreams and live happily ever after!

Self-Reflection Questions

1. What is it that you are looking for in a mate?

_____
_____
_____
_____
_____
_____
_____

2. What do you love about yourself that you would like to include in your online dating profile?

_____
_____
_____
_____
_____
_____
_____

3. What are the best and most recent photos of you? What do you love about them?

_____
_____
_____
_____
_____
_____
_____

4. How can you showcase your hobbies and talents in photos?

_____
_____
_____
_____
_____
_____
_____

5. What can you share in a private message with someone on an online dating site that will help you stand out?

_____
_____
_____
_____
_____
_____
_____

6. What can you do to avoid catfishing? How can you watch out for scams while still looking for love?

_____
_____
_____
_____
_____
_____
_____

7. What do you want to accomplish with online dating? Do you want to meet your soulmate, or are you looking for a causal relationship?

_____
_____
_____
_____
_____
_____
_____

CHAPTER 15

Summary – Self-Love Makeover

Practical Application

Faith

Self-Love – *if you don't have it, you need it!* Believe for it in your heart and manifest it in your life.

Self-Love is the ability to embrace who you are as a person fully. You don't only feel love for yourself, though. You back it up and prove it by acting and behaving in ways that honor that feeling. It's one thing to say you love yourself and an entirely different thing to live and breathe it.

Fitness

Get your head and your heart in the process. You've got what it takes to do the work.

The best way to embrace the concept of Self-Love is to focus on the six *"aspects of self"* that we have outlined here. Self-Love is a combination of:

- Self-Worthy
- Self-Aware
- Self-Care

- Self-Respect
- Self-Esteem
- Self-Growth

Finances

If you can commit, invest the time, treasure (money), and talents (your unique self) to increasing and manifesting these feelings, self-love will naturally occur.

Don't feel discouraged if you aren't feeling it yet, though. This isn't the kind of makeover you get at the makeup counter in a department store. This is the kind of makeover that many people spend their whole lives trying to achieve.

Self-love is naturally harder to come by for some of us. Past traumas, especially serious ones, can be nearly impossible to just "shake off." You might want to love yourself more, but then something holds you back. You might even do everything suggested in this book but still struggle to embrace who you are.

If this is the case, reach out to a professional that can help you process this trauma. There is no shame in getting a professional's opinion, especially when it concerns something as serious as your ability to love yourself.

Family and Friends

Along with the professional help you may seek or require for that matter, don't forget about the support of your family and friends.

Remember that family can be blood or chosen. Your family and friends will cheer you on, support and help you when needed.

No matter how easy (or hard) it is for you to accept that you are worthy of love, we applaud you for trying.

The steps you have taken in this section are sure to have a positive impact on your life.

Festivities

We hope reading this book leaves you feeling just as good about yourself as leaving the salon with an amazing new haircut or going out in that designer dress you've had your eyes on for ages.

You are worth it, after all.

So, celebrate, Y-O-U! Dance in the middle of the kitchen. Cook or purchase your favorite meal. Invite a bestie over and enjoy self-love made-over self.

Queue the music.

Prayer

God thank You for your loving kindness. Thank You for reminding us that a healthy love of self is encouraged and required. When we love ourselves well, we are better equipped to recognize the right love for us when it appears. Also, we are able to be better mothers, nurturers, life-givers to the gifts, the children that You have entrusted to our care. Help us love us better. Let it be so and so it is.

Promise

_____
_____
_____

Guidepost III – MONEY

Story – Daughters of Zelophehad's

Numbers 27:1-11
[7]"The claim of the daughters of Zelophehad is legitimate. You must give them a grant of land along with their father's relatives. Assign them the property that would have been given to their father". (New Living Translation)

Leaving a legacy for our children is important. However, on the pathway to leaving that legacy, we need to eat. We need to maintain a place to live. There are field trips. Sports. Plays. Lunches. Sleepovers. Clothes. Uniforms. Books. College applications. College. Tuition. And the lists go on and on.

We have needs. Our children have needs. Maslow's Hierarchy of Needs; basic needs. Those needs require resources, finances, money.

Zelophehad died and he had no sons. His daughters hadn't married yet and Jewish law at that point in time, didn't allow a father's inheritance to be passed to his daughters. Zelophehad's daughters fought for what was theirs.

They presented their case to Moses. Moses took their concern to God and God answered. Give them girls their money. That's my paraphrase for the verse above. Laughing hysterically out loud.

It was written in history and changed the trajectory of daughter's economic liberation for perpetuity.

What do you need to present to your High Priest and fight for? That promotion? A new job maybe?

CHAPTER 16

Not Just Money But Abundance

Some people equate financial success with abundance. Having enough money is a significant part of abundance, but there's much more to it.

Abundance is a mindset and a belief system. It's a way of viewing the world, the people in it, and yourself. It's making the decision to believe that the universe will provide, as long as you hold up your end of the bargain.

You can be wealthy and be alone. You can have money and be in poor health. You can be financially successful and be miserable. You can be the wealthiest person in the world and still not experience abundance.

Consider these ideas and experience abundance in your life:

1. Abundance is an attitude. Money is money, but abundance is a mindset. It's a decision to believe that you can have whatever you need, in the quantities you need it. It's the belief that there is always enough.

2. Abundance is having an excess of important resources. True abundance isn't just money. It's also

about having enough of the other necessary resources in your life. This can include things like free time, love, and happiness. Money is important, but there's much more to abundance than money.

3. Abundance is the belief that there is enough for everyone. Those obsessed with wealth are often competitive and believe that there's only a finite amount of wealth to be divided among everyone. Abundance is the belief that there's enough for everyone.

4. Abundance has a greater impact on happiness than wealth. Abundance greatly increases the likelihood of happiness. Great wealth is no more likely to make you happy than a decent middle-class income. There's research to support this idea. You can't make yourself happier by accumulating great wealth.

5. Abundance avoids attachment. Abundance lacks attachment. There's no reason to hold on tightly to what you have if you believe there will always be enough in the future. With an abundance mindset, you feel comfortable allowing everything to flow into and out of your life.

6. Abundance allows you to dream bigger. Abundance allows for the biggest of dreams to become a possibility in your mind. Money provides opportunities, but only for those things you can afford. Abundance takes the possibilities in your life to another level.

7. Abundance avoids resentment. With abundance, there's no reason to be jealous or resentful of someone else's success. The success of one person can't negatively impact the success of someone else.

8. Those with an abundant mindset are grateful. Gratitude is part of abundance. You can't experience abundance unless you're grateful for what you have. Gratitude creates the possibility of receiving even more in the future. How grateful are you right now?

9. Abundance leads to positive expectations. When you believe in abundance, you are positive about the future. You expect good things to happen and to continue happening.

How much abundance do you have in your life? How would you measure abundance? What does abundance mean to you? You can't acquire what you don't identify.

Resist the urge to believe that all of your challenges will be solved with money. Once your money issues are solved, you have a whole new set of problems to deal with. You just couldn't see them before.

For example, you don't care too much about your unreliable car if you're in the process of drowning in the lake. You don't see your loneliness as a problem if you're struggling to buy food each month. Money solves certain challenges, but there are more challenges waiting for you.

Abundance can solve far more challenges than money. Seek abundance in all forms. This is much more powerful than just a large bank account.

CHAPTER 17

Financial Realty Therapy

Welcome to Financial Therapy.

If your life is one financial challenge after another, financial therapy might be just what the doctor ordered. Over 75% of Americans list money as their primary source of stress. Financial therapy is a growing field and focuses on the emotional and psychological roots of financial behaviors that create financial stress.

For example, someone that grew up in poor surroundings might hoard money and be overly frugal. Overspending can be caused by stress or anxiety.

While some issues may be better left to the professionals, there are many financial issues amenable to self-therapy. After all, many overweight people are able to lose weight without a psychologist, dietitian, and personal trainer.

By addressing the beliefs, thoughts, and habits related to your financial life, it's possible to bring about real changes.

If you're not following through on the actions that you know would increase your financial stability, your beliefs are likely to blame.

Beliefs that inhibit financial results can come from many sources:

- Parents
- Teachers
- News
- Erroneous personal observation
- Childhood trauma related to family finances
- Books
- Personal experience throughout life

The source of the ineffective belief doesn't matter. But recognizing and addressing harmful money beliefs is very important to your financial progress.

Beliefs create and limit your reality.

It might only be a few faulty habits that are holding you back from the financial security that you desire.

How exciting is that?

How Your Beliefs Create and Limit Your Financial Reality

Your beliefs are the seeds that create your reality.

Your beliefs affect your thoughts, which affect your actions, which ultimately create your life circumstances. Changing your beliefs can be the most powerful way to alter your life. Altering your beliefs changes the entire cycle.

There are several ways that beliefs ultimately alter your financial behavior:

1. Beliefs influence your self-confidence. The set of be-

liefs you have about yourself, and your capabilities determines your level of self-confidence. In turn, your confidence affects your ability to learn and apply new financial habits.

- o Confidence also impacts your ability to pursue financial goals. If you're not confident in your ability to get results, you won't persevere.

2. Beliefs alter how you process information. Scientists have found that people use new information to support beliefs they already possess, rather than to form new beliefs. If you believe that you can't save money, you'll look for evidence to support that belief.

- o Information that is contrary to your beliefs is quickly discarded and ignored. This makes change especially challenging.

3. Beliefs create limits. It's almost impossible to rise above your beliefs. If you believe that you'll never be wealthy, you're right. If you believe you can't stick to a budget, you're right again. This is why it's so important to change your beliefs to viewpoints that support, rather than limit, you.

4. Beliefs affect results. If you don't think you can have a pleasant retirement, you're unlikely to save or learn about the various types of retirement accounts.

- o If you believe that money changes people for the worse, you won't take the steps to accumulate a significant amount.

Beliefs are the core of financial challenges. Enhanced beliefs lead to enhanced thoughts, actions, and results. Attacking your negative behaviors is a less effective route to success. Instead, focus on your beliefs and you're more likely to enjoy positive benefits from your efforts.

What are your beliefs about money?

Make a comprehensive list of your beliefs regarding money, both positive and negative.

Here are few examples of beliefs you may hold:

- I'll have to work really hard to make a lot of money.
- Making a lot of money will cut into my free time.
- I already have enough money.
- I don't need a budget.
- Money equals freedom.
- If I make too much money, my ex-spouse will take most of it.
- I wouldn't know what to do with a lot of money.
- Money makes the world go round.
- Good people don't care about having a lot of money.
- More money would solve all of my problems.

Take the time to make a complete list. You'll need it later.

There are many ways to change the course of your financial life. Addressing your beliefs is the most effective way to create the financial future you desire. With more supportive beliefs, it will be much easier to create the habits necessary to earn, save, and accumulate wealth.

CHAPTER 18

What it Takes to Achieve a State of Financial Health

Financial health isn't just how much money you make. That was discussed in the previous chapter. There are multiple components to financial prosperity and stability. There are people earning over a million dollars each year with desperate financial challenges.

The belief that income is all that matters is a limiting belief.

Do you have all of these financial components under control?

1. Budget. Whether you're earning minimum wage or running the most successful hedge fund the world has ever seen, a budget is important.

    o Know how much you're spending and where the money is being spent. There's no way around it. The information is valuable to you and provides boundaries that ensure your financial success.

2. An income that surpasses your bills. If your bills outpace your income, you're going to have financial woes. The most likely long-term outcome is bank-

ruptcy. Everyone would be wise to increase their income and lower their bills.

3. An emergency fund. Life is neither perfect nor predictable. Sooner or later, an unexpected expense will occur. Many families are only a few weeks away from being homeless if sudden unemployment or a major expense occurs.

4. A minimal amount of debt. No matter how much money you have or make, it's very easy to create more debt than you can handle.

    o Avoid debt whenever possible. Especially avoid debt to purchase items that are consumable or lose value.

5. Controlled spending. It's also easy to spend more than you make. Are you an impulsive shopper? Do you like to purchase items that are out of your income bracket?

6. Saving regularly. Are you saving a percentage of each and every paycheck? With regular saving, anyone can retire in style.

7. Investing your savings appropriately. Saving is great but leaving your money in a savings account is less than ideal. Do your investing activities address your needs? Are you saving for retirement?

8. The necessary insurance to prevent financial catastrophe. A serious illness, fire, or death can derail the best-laid plans.

Look back at your list of beliefs and note which of the

above items are influenced by your beliefs. You'll probably have several additional beliefs to add to your list now.

Remember, earning a lot of money is a great advantage, but it's not sufficient on its own to ensure financial security.

CHAPTER 19

Negative Money Beliefs and Money Blocks

Consider your list of your money beliefs. It's necessary to recognize which beliefs are negative and which are positive. Positive beliefs are those that allow you to positively affect the 8 components necessary for financial health.

Negative beliefs get in the way of addressing the 8 components.

Examples of beliefs that keep you poor:

1. Rich people are greedy. Some rich people are indeed greedy. But some poor people are greedy, too. Many rich people became rich through kindness and helping others. Whether or not you're greedy is up to you.

2. I don't deserve to be wealthy. Everyone that creates value deserves to be wealthy. If you have a minimum wage job or spend the day sitting on the couch, you can change your financial circumstances by creating value and charging the world for it.

3. I'll have to do a lot of things I don't like to become wealthy. While doing things that others don't like to do can be a faster way to wealth, there are numer-

ous ways to accumulate wealth. At least one of them would be enjoyable for you.

4. My friends won't like me if I'm rich. It's common to find new friends as your life situation evolves. Some of your friends might not like the fact that you're rich. But your true friends will be happy for you. Every change in life has the potential to influence everything else.

    o Many CEOs and other wealthy folks still have the same friends from elementary school. You can choose to do the same.

5. Money is the root of all evil. The actual quote is "The love of money is the root of all evil." Money doesn't create negative situations. Money is just a piece of paper, or a number attached to a bank account.

    o Money provides opportunity. It's your choice whether the actions you take are positive or negative.

6. I can't be spiritual and have a lot of money. Many religions espouse the belief that being poor is somehow looked upon kindlier by the great powers that be. But if you were looking to convert a population that was 99.9% dirt-poor, you'd probably say the same thing.

    o Having money gives you more opportunities to be good to yourself and others. It can also free up your time to engage in more spiritual activities.

7. I'm disrespecting my parents if I make more money

than they do. Most parents would be thrilled to see their child doing so well.

8. It's hard to make a lot of money. It can be hard to make any amount of money. Most people with moderate incomes complain about work. If you're going to work anyway, why not make a lot of money while you're at it?

    o With the appropriate habits in place, it's not too difficult to enhance your career, save more, spend less, and invest more wisely.

9. If I had a lot of money, I'd probably just lose it anyway. Keeping money is as much of a skill as earning and saving it. There are plenty of resources that can help you learn how to handle money wisely.

    o The belief that you'll end up where you started will prevent you from taking any meaningful action.

10. I shouldn't have more money than I need. Everything in life is easier with a buffer. Imagine having more time and love than you need. Having more money than you "need" is comforting and opens up many possibilities that simply don't exist without a surplus of funds.

    o It's much easier to make a career change or go back to school.

    o You can afford to send your child to Harvard instead of the local community college.

    o You're better prepared for any financial catastrophe.

o The belief that you shouldn't have more money than you need to survive will lead to surviving instead of thriving.

Do you have any of these common beliefs about money or yourself? If you hold beliefs that inhibit your ability to address the components of a healthy financial situation, your challenge will be greater than necessary. You'll sabotage yourself by neglecting the habits necessary to achieve financial happiness.

CHAPTER 20

Positive Money Beliefs

There are also beliefs that will speed you along the path to financial independence. These positive habits make it easier to have a positive financial future.

These beliefs can make you rich:

1. Money results from providing value to the world. It doesn't matter how smart or educated you are. It doesn't matter what you look like. The universe isn't out to get you. If you provide value and charge people for it, you will receive a corresponding level of money.

    o Brain surgeons make more money than your average store clerk because the surgeon is providing more value. A CEO of a large corporation earns more than a brain surgeon for the same reason.

2. Money provides freedom and choice. Money is great for solving problems and providing you with options. Maybe money can't buy you love, but enough of it can fix a bad transmission, buy a ticket to Fiji, or allow you to play golf all day instead of working.

3. I can help others with my money. After your own needs have been tended to, you have the ability to help others with their challenges or assist them in attaining their goals.

4. My financial freedom will happen when I have effective beliefs, thoughts, and habits. It's not necessary to do anything spectacular. Simple actions, taken on a regular basis, will result in great wealth. But it all starts with your beliefs.

5. Saving money is easy and enjoyable. How would your savings activities change if you believed this?

6. A budget is easy to create and follow. If you can't seem to create or stick with a budget, this belief will help.

7. I only buy things I need. How would your bank account look if you lived this belief?

There are numerous others, but you get the idea. Do you have more positive or negative beliefs about money? Can you see how your beliefs about money are affecting your financial situation?

If you want to enhance your finances, eliminating negative beliefs and replacing them with positive beliefs is an effective plan of attack.

CHAPTER 21

How to Change a Belief

There are many ways to address harmful beliefs and replace them with positive. Many times, all that's required is a little attention and an open mind.

Many of our beliefs are created during childhood and are never questioned. At one time, you believed in the Easter Bunny. So, it's likely that you have several beliefs about money that are impractical, too.

The experts can't agree whether beliefs can be changed in an instant or whether it takes a significant amount of time. By like the old Chinese proverb states, "The best time to plant a tree was twenty years ago. The second-best time is today."

Neuro-Linguistic Programming

John Grindler and Richard Bandler developed Neuro-linguistic programming (NLP) in the 1970s. You're probably familiar with Tony Robbins, who made the technology popular.

Though there are many facets to NLP, we're most interested in the use of language and perception to change beliefs. For instance, if you imagine something that frightens you, the way you imagine it has an impact. There are an infinite number of ways to think about a spider, for example.

If the image of a spider in our mind is very large and colorful, it will have a different impact on your emotions than an image that's small and lacking color.

The characteristics of a mental image are called submodalities. These include the visual, auditory, and kinesthetic details of a mental image.

Follow this process to change a belief with NLP:

1. Identify a belief you'd like to change. Let's pretend you believe that you can't save enough money each month to ever make a difference.

2. Consider an old belief that you no longer consider to be true. Perhaps you once believed in Santa Claus or that your high school girlfriend was the only woman you'd ever love. Notice the submodalities of this once-held belief.

    o Are you in the image or viewing it like you're watching a movie?

    o Is it in color or black and white?

    o Is there a border around the image?

    o Is the image centered?

    o What do you hear?

    o Can you feel anything? Hot? Cold? Sick to your stomach?

3. Think of something you know to be true. It could be the belief that Christmas is on December 25th or that a dropped bowling ball will fall. Take note of the submodalities for this belief.

4. Think of a belief that you'd like to add. For our example, it might be the belief that every penny saved is adding to your fortune. Find the most advantageous counter-belief to the belief in step #1. Notice the submodalities.

5. Eliminate the belief in step #1. Take the submodalities you found in step #2 and apply them to the image in step #1. You're applying the mental characteristics of a belief you no longer hold to the belief you'd like to eliminate.

6. Now alter the submodalities of the belief you'd like to add to match those of the belief in step #4. Make your desired belief have the same mental characteristics of the belief you know to be 100% absolutely true.

7. Test. How do you feel about the original belief and the new belief? Can you feel a change? The ultimate test is to observe your behavior. If you behavior changes, you know you're on the right track.

Many people find this process highly effective. It's possible to change a belief quickly with NLP. If NLP doesn't seem to work for you, though, there are other options.

Change a Belief With Logic

Humans are thinkers, and we can use logic to our advantage. Beliefs are funny things. Though we can be influenced to believe anything, we're ultimately the creators of our beliefs. You can't see or touch a belief in the real world. No one can give you a belief you don't accept.

Use the power of logic to shake the foundation of your harmful beliefs:

1. Choose a belief you'd like to change. For this example, we'll look at the belief, "Money is the root of all evil."
2. Where did this belief come from? Did it come from your parents? A minister? A teacher? Neighbor? Did you read that money is the root of all evil? Knowing the origin can help to change the belief.
3. Is this source an expert? In reality, only a person that's had a lot of money would have the experience to make such a statement.
    - Your parents might have had authority over you, but did they really have authority and expertise when it came to being wealthy?
4. What is another possible explanation? It's possible that money is the root of all evil, but what other explanation could there be? Maybe your current belief is just one possible explanation.
    - Maybe you just heard that money is the root of all evil so many times you've believed it without questioning it.
    - Maybe money gives evil people the chance to be evil. But does that mean that all people are evil?
    - Have you ever actually seen money causing evil?

Money is just an object. Have you ever seen another object create evil?

- o Is it possible that the reasons for this belief only exist in your mind and not in the real world?

5. Realize we form many beliefs in childhood that fail to hold up to examination. It's understandable why a child forms certain beliefs under the conditions of childhood. Those in similar situations would likely draw the same conclusions.

6. Can you see that any of the other interpretations could also be "the truth?" So what is the truth? It's whatever you choose it to be. You are the creator, and your belief is merely your creation. You interpret ideas and experiences and assign value to these things. Find an interpretation that makes sense but also works for, rather than against, you.

Faulty beliefs can be easy to change because they have the disadvantage of being incorrect. Most of the beliefs that stand in your way can't stand up to scrutiny. Examine your beliefs around money and put them to the test.

Cost – Benefit Analysis

You've undoubtedly made lists in the past listing the pluses and minuses of your available options. Why don't do the same with your beliefs? If you realize what a particular belief is costing you, you'll have greater motivation to address it. It's also important to realize what you gain from beliefs that seem to be holding you back.

Follow these steps to analyze the cost and benefit of your challenging money beliefs:

1. Choose a belief you wish to change. Consider the belief, "I'll never make $100,000 per year."

2. What is this belief costing me? A few examples might include:

   o If I don't believe I can make $100,000, it's unlikely I ever will.

   o I'll be stuck in my current income bracket for the rest of my life.

   o I don't have hope for the future.

   o I'll never be able to buy the house I've always wanted.

   o I'll have to work until I'm much older than I'd like.

3. How is this belief unreasonable? Few things in life are 100% true all of the time. How is this belief ridiculous?

   o I can't predict the future, so how could I possibly know how much I'll make someday?

   o If I have the skills and work hard, than my current limits are irrelevant.

   o Other people with fewer skills, less intelligence, and less education have made over $100,000 per year. In fact, some of the wealthiest people in the world dropped out of high school.

   o There's nothing magical about $100,000. It's just a round number that looks good to my brain.

4. What do I gain by holding this belief? In most cases,

you'll find that seemingly harmful beliefs have an advantage. That advantage is often avoiding fear or getting to be lazy. If you don't think you can make more money, you don't have to try. Harmful beliefs are often excuses to avoid taking action.

5. What would I gain by adopting a more helpful belief? How would you benefit if you believed you could make $100,000 in the future?

    o I would greatly increase the likelihood of reaching this income level.

    o I would have hope and enthusiasm for the future.

    o I would work harder, and my job would be more secure from my increased effort and contribution.

6. Create an affirmation. State your new belief in a positive, present way. "I earn $100,000 per year."

    o Repeat the affirmation 20 times each morning and evening while in bed.

    o Avoid discounting the effectiveness of affirmations. Try a simple experiment and apply affirmations to a simple task you routinely avoid, perhaps getting up the first time your alarm goes off. When you hear the alarm, turn it off and repeat, "Getting up, getting up, getting up" over and over again. You'll find it much easier to put your feet on the floor!

One of these three methods will work better than the others for you. The key is to try all three. Changing your beliefs takes effort. Merely understanding the processes won't accomplish anything. It's necessary to apply them consistently.

CHAPTER 22

A Simple Plan of Action

1. Determine the part of your financial life that's causing the most grief. Suppose that you have no retirement savings.

2. Make a list of the beliefs that are having the greatest negative impact. Which belief is hurting you the most?

    o I'll have plenty of time later.

    o I'm too young to worry about it.

    o I have to buy a house first.

    o I won't live long enough to enjoy it.

    o I can't afford to save money now for something I won't need for 40 years.

    o It's too complicated for me.

    o I'll inherit all the money I could ever need.

    o The amount I'm able to save won't make a difference.

3. Address them one at a time. Pick the belief that you think is creating the biggest obstacle and apply one

of the techniques to eliminate the belief and create a new, more supportive belief.

4. Keep going until your behavior matches your wishes. It's possible to feel better but not take action. Keep going until you're taking real action. You might have to try all three techniques to have an impact.

5. Continue addressing all of your beliefs that don't support your financial future. This will take time, but it's time well spent.

A few simple steps taken each day will have a very positive impact in the future.

Start by taking the first step.

CHAPTER 23

Finding A Job In The New Economy

If you're currently embarking on a job-seeking journey, it's wise to use every possible avenue to obtain your next position. Taking advantage of the wide range of new strategies to land your dream job can enrich your possibilities.

Before you begin looking for new employment, update your resume to ensure it highlights your professional skills. Inventory your personal and social skills to determine if you'd like to make some positive changes that could help you obtain the position you desire.

To bridge the gap between employment and unemployment, use temporary solutions to keep cash flowing into your household.

Because of the vast opportunities that exist on the internet, consider online employment.

Use online networking, both professionally and socially to expand your field of contacts as a way of finding work. Even volunteering can increase your contacts, exposure, and work skills that can lead to a new job.

Update Your Resume to Show off Your Skills

If you need a job quickly, the first thing to do is keep a level head. Build momentum, one step at a time.

Take a good look at your work credentials. Update your resume.

Follow these steps to update, enhance, and polish your resume:

1. Spend a morning thoroughly reading through your resume. Add relevant information that best reflects your professional persona.
    - Re-word anything that sounds awkward.
    - Focus on clearly defining your skills.
    - Highlight your training, education, and experience that shows expertise in your field.

2. Use action verbs when describing the work you've done in the past. Use words like these on your resume:
    - Resume experts recommend using present-tense verbs to describe your prior work tasks when editing your job descriptions.

3. Format your resume to make it memorable. Your goal is to have a resume that's easy to read yet stands out from the pile.
    - Utilize bold print to set off the names of prior jobs you've held.
    - Include your contact information at the top of

your resume to facilitate easy and quick contact by those who review your credentials.

4. Limit your resume to two pages if at all possible. Narrow it down to the education and experience which best show your qualifications for the position you seek.

   o However, keep a copy of your "long" resume on your computer to access in the event you need to later detail other experiences you've had.

5. Do a final proofing and editing to ensure your resume is in tip-top shape. Run a spell-check.

   o Then, re-read the entire document to catch any grammatical or spelling errors that your spell-check may not identify.

Re-doing your resume is important to your job search. Update any facts about your job history using action verbs in the present tense.

Use professional formatting to make your resume shine. Keep it to two pages if possible. Then, do an overall, final editing and proofing to ensure your resume is ready to go.

Take an Inventory of Your Personal and Social Skills

When you're job seeking, examining your personal skills is a smart thing to do. Are you open to others, or do you come across as shy or disinterested?

Practicing these social skills can help you find employment:

1. Your personality plays a major role in determining how you relate to others. Even so, you can make efforts to be more outgoing when you're around people you don't know well.

2. Do you establish new contacts easily? Introducing yourself to every person present whom you haven't yet met is a wonderful step to take in a social situation, particularly when you're looking for employment.

3. Make an effort to be friendly. In new social situations, if you're friendly and easy to get along with, chances are better that those contacts will remember you.

    o If they remember you favorably, they may consider you when they need to hire someone.

    o Because your contacts also have contacts, every good impression counts!

Taking an inventory of your personal and social skills will enlighten you about how you relate to others. Establishing new contacts easily, going out of your way to be friendly and considering the "reach" of every person you meet are effective aspects of any job search.

Utilize Temporary Solutions for Finding Work

Sometimes, looking for work can be daunting, especially when more than a few weeks go by without seeing any real interest from employers. Be ready and willing to utilize temporary solutions to find work.

Use these strategies to help bridge the gap between past employment and your future permanent job:

1. Make contact in person with the temporary services offices in your local area. Using temporary employment services is a great way to keep money coming in as you embark on a journey to find the perfect job.

    o Going in person to your local temporary services office will provide an opportunity to "practice" your job interviewing skills.

    o A variety of temporary work businesses might be available in your area including Elite Staffing, Kelly Services, AppleOne, Randstad, Aerotek, and Manpower.

    o Because of the number of temporary services organizations that might have locations in your area, the possibilities of obtaining a job through agencies are good.

    o In some cases, you might even find a permanent job through placement by a temp service.

2. Consider quick methods of making cash by selling your services. If you've updated your resume and applied at all the temporary services in your area, there might be a brief period when you still don't have work.

    o During periods of unemployment, create your own work.

    o How? Make a list of all the skills you can do for others, like:

- Mow lawns, trim bushes, or sweep porches and walkways
- Sewing, knitting, and mending
- Wash cars
- Use a power washer on houses, driveways, and walkways
- Clean out garages and basements
- Clean and organize pantries and closets
- Painting - interior and exterior
- Hang pictures
- Clean houses
- Wash windows
- Dog-walking
- Baby-sitting
- Care for houses or pets when their owners are gone
- Handy-man tasks like light home repairs
- Personal shopping or running errands (pick up medications, pay bills for others, grocery shopping, and deliveries)

Spend some time thinking up your own list of services you can provide to others for a charge. Availing yourself of temporary work solutions will relieve some of the pressure during an employment search.

Going in person to your local temporary services offices and offering services in your neighborhood or to people you know are wonderful temporary jobs to make money. Be creative when it comes to doing temporary work to keep you afloat until you snag your next big job.

Explore Online Employment

There's a whole world of employment available through the internet. Virtual assisting, performing professional services for others, and completing pay-per-project work are all effective strategies of working online from home.

1. Become a virtual assistant. Virtual assistants provide office support and back-up to business using their own computers from their homes. They perform tasks such as responding to emails and other customer service, managing projects, online content management, and more.

2. Sell your writing, graphic design, or other professional services on the internet. A wealth of websites offer online opportunities to get paid for your talents. Can you write? Are you a pro with Photoshop or other software programs? Online business owners often hire freelancers to perform tasks they don't have the time, skills, or desire to do themselves.

    o Sites such as LinkedIn, Indeed, and Monster allow you to post your resume and work skills. Thousands of businesses use resources such as these to find professionals to whom they can outsource various projects. You can also bid on specific projects for those requesting help.

    o Forums, like The Warrior Forum, have large sub-forums dedicated to bringing business owners and skills providers together for mutual benefit. Many freelancers offer their services here and find there is no shortage of business owners willing to hire them.

o Avoid posting your resume or accepting work from any sites that require you to pay them to find you a job.

3. Full-time positions are also available online. Take the time to research major companies to see if they offer online options for working. In this age of technology, telecommuting, or working from home, is a rapidly growing industry.

Explore your online opportunities for jobs. Consider doing virtual assisting, web writing or pay-per-project work online. You might find a job you can do from your own home.

Access Online Networking to Find a Job

Sites such as LinkedIn, Facebook and others allow you access to thousands of potential employers. Survey several of the professional networking websites and see what you think.

If you typically work in the business world, you have the most to gain by joining some professional and social networking sites. It's easy! Plus, most of them are free to join.

Professional Networking

On the web, you'll find numerous networking sites devoted to individuals of like professions joining together to help and guide one another. Some professional networking sites, such as LinkedIn, encourage people from all different professions to sign up at the site to broaden professional contacts.

Explore the LinkedIn website and then join it to expand your job horizons. LinkedIn is a business network that allows you to interact with former colleagues as well as new people in your field of expertise.

- When looking for work, all you have to do is click on "looking for a job" at the LinkedIn website and a list of current open positions appears.
- In fact, at the time of this writing, over 55,000 jobs were available on LinkedIn.
- One benefit of LinkedIn is that you have access to professionals in your field who can offer advice and networking strategies to further your career.
- Human Resources managers seeking new employees often search through LinkedIn memberships, so it just makes sense to set up a profile there to show off your professional skills and talents.

Other business networking sites where you can find support, guidance, information and other professionals like you are:

- Career Builder
- eCademy
- Networking for Professionals

When you're trying to obtain employment, utilize all the tools within your power, especially online business networking sites, to increase your chances of landing a desirable job.

Social Networking

Social networking is a "must have" strategy when you're job-seeking. Utilized by millions of people, Facebook is "the" social network to be a part of, especially when you're trying to gain employment.

When it comes to job seeking, the more contacts you have, the better. Facebook can easily expand your field of contacts.

Consider these job-searching benefits of Facebook:

- Facebook allows you to take a look at your "friends' friends," which could lead you to making a connection that results in finding a job.
- Also, of great value at Facebook is that, with the information in your profile, you can advertise that you're looking for work.
- You can also ask all of your Facebook friends to post that you're involved in a job search.
- The potential to reach hundreds of people regarding your job search is possible with Facebook.

Although Facebook is the largest social network, you can find the same benefits in others as well. Some other popular social networking sites you might want to join to expand your employment search are Twitter and LinkedIn.

Joining various professional and social networking websites is a wise strategy to help you find employment. At the very least, join LinkedIn and Facebook to get your name noticed by hundreds of potential employers.

Volunteer to Find a Job

Although it may seem odd, becoming a volunteer might open all kinds of employment doors for you. You'll meet some new people when you volunteer.

You'll make contact with at least one business (the one you're volunteering for) and possibly others, depending on the type of volunteer work you do.

Even more relevant, volunteering is your best opportunity to literally show people what you can do.

Where to Volunteer

The types of businesses and organizations where you can volunteer are wide and varied:

1. Social service agencies are a good place to start when you're looking to volunteer. Social service agencies such as Salvation Army, Goodwill, Boys and Girls Club, YMCA and YWCA usually need all types of assistance.

   o Such publicly funded agencies cannot afford to pay employees to complete all the tasks that need to be completed. These agencies, therefore, utilize volunteers to help accomplish their missions.

   o From addressing envelopes to sweeping floors, stocking shelves, or answering the phones, volunteering at a social service organization will increase your potential business contacts and expand your skills and experience in ways you can't imagine.

2. Other businesses that utilize volunteers are healthcare organizations, such as hospitals and clinics. In hospitals, you might deliver newspapers, magazines, and flowers to patients or help with admis-

sion, reception or messenger duties. Hospitals have so many departments and programs that you just might meet your next "paying" boss by volunteering at a hospital.

3. Churches also need volunteers. Consider your own church as a place to volunteer. Does it have a congregation of 400, 500, or more? You stand to come into regular contact with many people if you volunteer at your own church. Whether it's answering the phones or picking up around the building, you expand your repertoire by volunteering at a church.

Political and Social Activism

If volunteering at social service agencies, healthcare facilities, or your church doesn't appeal to you, consider a political or social activism group. You'll make contacts and learn valuable skills when you volunteer to work for a political party or a social cause.

Get active in a cause you believe in. Becoming involved in a political or social platform in which you're already interested will enrich you in many ways, not to mention possibly open up possibilities for your next job.

Whether it's MADD (Mothers against Drunk Driving) or Susan G. Komen for the Cure, put your true efforts into doing something of personal value.

What better way to encounter a variety of self-motivated, working people than through political and social activism?

Learn New Things By Volunteering

Another concrete advantage to volunteering is that you'll get the opportunity to learn new skills and further develop your talents. Expanding what you know is a great way to better prepare yourself for your next job.

After all, volunteering provides you with free, on-the-job training. Soak up everything you can from a volunteer experience. There's no other way to feel more appreciated while learning valuable skills. Consider volunteering as the new way to gain knowledge and training while in between jobs.

Show Others What You Can Do By Volunteering

Volunteering provides opportunities for you to "show off." Demonstrating important work ethics like showing up a few minutes early or taking notes on the job will lead others to notice you. You can show that you'll do what you're expected to do, evidence a cheerful mood, and make every effort to be helpful.

If you want to demonstrate what a smart and effective worker you are, consider volunteering.

Regardless of where you decide to volunteer, doing so will increase your chances of finding work. Learning new skills and having the forum to show others your skills and talents are smart ways to take advantage of your spare time. All the way around, volunteering is the way to go if you're looking for work.

A Wise Philosophy to Help You Find Work

Even though it's important to survey your education, skills and experience when you're looking for a job, there's something else important to consider: "It's not what you know; it's who you know."

So, what does this statement really mean when it comes to job-seeking?

1. Although your skills, experience, and education are relevant, even more so is who you know and who they know. In other words, when you're involved in a job search, think about all the people you know.

    o Who do you know that owns their own business? Do they need help?

    o Who do you know that just took a new job? Does their employer need more people?

    o Maybe you know someone who works for an employer that hires professionals for temporary work or outsources some projects to freelancers.

2. Remember your online contacts. The same mantra applies to your online neighborhood - it's not so much what you know, but who you know (and who they know).

    o Most people have more online contacts than they do "in-person" contacts.

    o Who you know online might determine your next job.

    o Avoid under-estimating the value of your online contacts when it comes to job-seeking.

Keep this philosophy in mind when you're looking for work. It's very likely that your contacts, online or otherwise, will lead you to your next job.

Follow Up On Any Communication

Regardless of whom you make contact within your job search, it's imperative to perform some type of follow-up with them afterward.

Why? It shows good manners and a professional demeanor to thank a person for taking the time to talk with you. Good manners make a good impression. Also, when you follow-up, you remind the employer about you and your work talents.

When an employer remembers you favorably, he's more likely to think of you when he's deciding who to hire for his open positions.

Choose any of these ways to perform a follow-up communication:

- Telephone call
- Written letter
- Email

Consistently provide follow-up communications with those you contact regarding your job search. People will remember your good manners. Plus, following up demonstrates your stellar work ethic.

Take Advantage of Your Time Off

Remember how, when you were working, you just couldn't find the energy or time to fit in opportunities to increase your skills? Now, you've got the luxury of time to use to propel you forward in your life.

Make your time off count by getting training, gaining knowledge and developing new work skills:

3. Strengthen your computer skills. If you have a few spare hours, sharpening your typing skills is the thing to do these days.

    o Because the vast majority of jobs require computer work of some kind, use this time to improve your computer skills. You can use free online typing websites such as Good Typing and Typing Web to improve your keyboarding skills. Or learn new techniques of using Microsoft Office by researching step-by-step video tutorials.

4. Take a class. It's a perfect time to expand your knowledge. You may qualify for more scholarships and other funds if you're between jobs.

5. Seek out any other training or education you desire. Take advantage of the time you have when you have it. Sign up right away to expand your professional skills and knowledge.

Use your time off to expand your professional horizons. Sharpen job skills, take a class or get more education and training. When that next job opportunity comes along, you'll be ready.

Finding a job isn't always easy. Nevertheless, you can

make your job search a journey that revives and enriches you in many ways. Open up to the many job-seeking opportunities surrounding you and you'll find your best job yet!

CHAPTER 24

Tips To Negotiate Higher Starting Salary

In life, everything is negotiable and starting salaries in a new position are no exception. As a knowledgeable professional, you have experience under your belt and other valuable skills that employers should be charged a premium for utilizing.

Give yourself your worth by negotiating your starting salary within a new company. Not only will it put you on a better financial footing, but it'll also make you seem like an ambitious businessperson.

Follow the tips below in order to confidently and successfully negotiate a higher starting salary:

1. Mum is the word. If you're too forthcoming about your salary requirements, you may come off as desperate. *Desperation is something that turns an employer off - big time.*

    o Furthermore, you may lock yourself into a lower starting salary simply because you've given too much information about your salary requirements before the employer has even had a chance to assess your value.

- If your interview is truly impressive, the person interviewing you may give you their absolute highest salary offering immediately simply to ensure that you'll take the position.

2. It's not about you. Companies hire employees based on what the candidate has to offer the company, not the other way around. Yet, so many candidates choose to exaggerate the fact of how they've always dreamt of landing this job, what the position will mean to them, and more.

    - Excitement is good. But, *acting too exuberant can cause the interviewer to perceive you as immature.* Rather than focusing on what a life-changing experience this is for you, make it known that you're right for the job because you have a proven track record of saving money, increasing profits, improving employee performance, or some other *benefit for the company.*

    - If the interviewer can see you as an equal counterpart, rather than a giddy newbie, only then will the discussion of salary requirements be pertinent. Also, your assertiveness in this high-pressure situation *gives the interviewer a glimpse as to how you will handle high-pressure situations in the workplace.*

3. Don't jump at the first offer. Unless you've blown the socks off of the employer, it's unlikely that the first offer you're presented with is their absolute best. It's possible, but not probable.

    - If an employer says they're ready to offer you $45,000, keep cool, calm and collected - even if the offer is much lower or higher than you were expecting. Wait a few seconds to see if they adjust the offer, and if not, counter with a higher figure.

- o There's no need to play hardball, just be firm in your approach. If you're offered $45,000 and you know you're worth $55,000, ask for $55,000. The worst that can happen is that you'll be told that $45,000 is their absolute maximum budget. *You can still take the offer as long as it's on the table.*

4. Take the offer. If all of your negotiation tactics have failed and you needed the job yesterday, take the offer. But ask the employer to analyze your performance within six months in order to possibly negotiate a raise.

- o With an offer like this, the employer has nothing to lose. If you are truly as good as you think you are, you'll be able to slash their costs, improve staff productivity, or increase sales, and he will be able to afford to offer you a raise.

Negotiation is all about the legwork. Do your research on the company, their current salary offerings, and the average salary in your locality.

If this is your first time negotiating a salary, it can be daunting. But, **you have nothing to lose.** If the job is being offered to you anyways, why not try to make it as profitable as can be?

CHAPTER 25

Secondary Sources of Income

Do you have some extra time and need another source of income? **There are several ways to generate a secondary source of income without leaving the comfort of your own home.** It's surprising how many home employment opportunities exist. Anyone with a few hours to spare can earn extra money.

Check out these ways to stay at home and earn money in your free time:

1. Freelancing. With the capabilities of the internet and associated technologies, working from home is a snap. Whether your talent is writing, graphics, building websites, or voiceover work, there's no end to the amount of work available for a freelancer.

    o *No matter what your skills might be, there's someone out there looking for you.* Check out one of the many freelance websites to get started.

2. Telemarketing. Any place with a telephone is suitable for your telemarketing headquarters. It's a job that few enjoy, so there are usually employers looking for callers. If you have a pleasant voice and can

deal with rejection, telemarketing can be an easy and flexible way to earn some money.

3. Grow and sell vegetables. Okay, you might have to leave home to do this. On the other hand, you might be able to convince someone else to sell them for you at the local farmer's market. Seeds are very inexpensive. Mother Nature will take care of the rest, minus weeding.

4. Make scrapbooks. Not everyone has the skill to make a custom scrapbook. *Create scrapbooks for those who are unable or unwilling to do it themselves.* A few supplies are all you need to get started.

    o Begin with offering your scrapbooking service to family, friends, and neighbors. You might be able to generate enough referrals to stay busy without additional advertising.

5. Data Entry. Most jobs pay for each entry rather than by the hour. It's a great job if you have a few spare minutes here and there. It's super flexible and can work around any schedule. With focus and fast fingers, you can generate a reasonable income.

6. Tutoring. *Part-time tutors can make $30 or more per hour.* You might have to brush up on your geometry or Latin, but tutoring can be a lucrative way to spend your free time.

7. Translate. Are you skilled in a second language? There are many opportunities to translate conversations and documents. While certifications are required to translate for large companies and gov-

ernment agencies, they're totally unnecessary for translating a love letter or a conversation on Skype.

8. Rent out a room. If you have the space to spare, rent out a room. A good roommate can be a blessing and help you cover the bills. It might help your social life, too.

9. Host a party. There are parties for Tupperware, candles, and numerous other types of products. While these parties are typically held in the homes of others, host the parties yourself.

    o *You could also allow your friends to use your home as a party location, and then keep a percentage of the profits.*

10. Sell ad space on a personal blog. Create a blog and then sell ads on your website. You can sell the ad space directly or sign up with Google AdSense. With Google, they'll post relevant ads for you, and you'll receive money whenever someone clicks on the ad.

Whether you're in financial pain or just need an activity to fill your spare time, a secondary or part-time source of income could be the solution. Someone almost certainly has a need that fits your skill set perfectly. Find them and provide your services. It might be the most enjoyable money you'll ever earn.

CHAPTER 26

Summary: Money

Practical Application

Faith

Are your beliefs about money supporting you or acting like a boat anchor? We often know what to do but struggle to follow through and take the appropriate action. Faulty beliefs inhibit your ability to address your finances successfully.

These beliefs alter your perception, behavior, and ultimately, your financial future.

Fitness

It's important to determine these beliefs and evaluate them. Consider how these beliefs negatively impact your financial future. What would you gain by eliminating these beliefs and instilling more helpful beliefs?

The fortitude to change your money beliefs can be accomplished by a variety of methods.

Finances

Finding the optimal method is a matter of trial and error.

It's important to get started immediately. Financial challenges rarely happen overnight. The cure will take time, too.

Invest the time. Invest the money if necessary to meet with a financial planner or someone that is great at budgeting.

Family and Friends

Give yourself financial therapy. Change your money beliefs and change your life. But you don't have to go it alone. Ask for help.

Look in your family and friendship circle. What you need may be closer than you think and may not "cost" your money. It may only cost you some of your time.

Festivities

Celebrate this milestone, within budget of course. Better yet, celebrate by opening a savings account. Setting an amount, you would like to save from each paycheck. Now that's a party watching your money grow!

Prayer

Thank You, God, for being a Provider. Thank You for opening doors of opportunity for me to walk through. That You for granting me strength to knock on doors, submit applications, and ask for what I'm worth. Thank you for giving me ideas to earn additional income without sacrificing my family. Thank you that I invest wisely, my money grows, I provide abundantly for my family, and I leave an inheritance. Let it be so and so it is.

Promise

Guidepost IV - Belief Systems

Story – Wisdom

All 31 Books
30"I [Wisdom] was the architect at His side. I was His constant delight, rejoicing always in His presence. 31And how happy I was with the world He created; how I rejoiced with the human family!" Proverbs 8:30-31 (New Living Translation)

I learned the benefits of reading one book of Proverbs a day. All 31 books are choked full of insight.

To set the intention of the fourth and final Guidepost, the more challenging deep dive into crushing self-limiting beliefs, Wisdom will be an affable companion.

Proverbs 8 details how Wisdom was present when God was speaking the earth and humankind into being. When God breathed into us, Wisdom was there and oversaw the masterpiece that has lasted ages.

The work we are doing to achieve our love and money goals, guilt-free and stress-free makes it necessary for us to conquer the final frontier. Our self-limiting beliefs.

Now we tear down those beliefs that haven't served us to our divine greatness. Now we rebuild a strong foundation for our "next", "bigger', "better", "healthy", "prosperous", today, and tomorrows to come.

"I, Wisdom, live together with good judgment. I know where to discover knowledge and discernment." Proverbs 8:12 (New Living Translation)

CHAPTER 27

No More Limits! Overcoming Your Self-Limiting Beliefs

We've talked about self-love and self-limiting beliefs. We've also talked about money, financial therapy, abundance, and the impacts of self-limiting beliefs. Finally, once and for all, it's time for no more limits!

Limiting beliefs are conscious or subconscious beliefs that hold you back in some way. They are ideas that limit you. Thoughts that keep you from reaching your full love and money potential.

These beliefs are often burned deeply into us and they restrict us from blooming into who we were truly meant to be.

All of us have limiting beliefs. Sometimes these beliefs originate in our childhood, instilled into us by our parents or friends. Other times these beliefs are the result of trauma we experience. Sometimes there is no obvious explanation for where these beliefs come from.

Whatever the case, these beliefs are damaging to us. They keep us from achieving our hopes, dreams, and goals.

They make us fearful and hesitant. They stop us from taking action. They even affect our relationships with others.

If we wish to achieve our true love and money potential, we must destroy the limiting beliefs that are holding us back.

We must be set free from the lies and falsehoods that we believe, both about ourselves and about the world. We must learn to see things as they truly are rather than as we think they are.

If we truly want to fly in life, to rise to our true potential, to fly to great heights, then we must leave behind the limiting beliefs that hold us back.

In this section, you'll discover 14 common destructive limiting beliefs that keep us from achieving all that we want to achieve.

We'll talk about common ideas around that limiting belief, how to rewrite the limiting belief into one that empowers you, specific action steps to take, and affirmations that will help destroy the limiting belief and instill your new, empowering belief.

Each of these chapters contains important action tips to help you learn and use these valuable strategies. Be sure to go through all the self-limiting beliefs with an open mind and try out the techniques. Remember, nothing happens until you take action.

Ready?

Let's dive in.

CHAPTER 28

Limiting Belief #1: I Don't Have Enough Time

Story – The 10 Virgins
Matthew 25:1-13
[10]"But while they were gone to buy oil, the bridegroom came. Then those who were ready went in with him to the marriage feast, and the door was locked." (New Living Translation)

If you're like most people, you're extremely busy. You've got projects to work on, things to do around the house, people to spend time with, administrative tasks like paying bills, and a thousand emails to answer.

You're so busy that you feel like you don't have enough time to do the things that really matter to you. To focus on your dreams. To really achieve your goals.

You feel like you're running in a thousand different directions without really making much progress on anything.

Put simply, you feel like there isn't enough time in the day and week to do what really matters. You think to yourself, *"If only I had more time, then I could do things I really wanted. If I had more hours in the day, I could get more things done."*

And when you look around, you see that all your friends and coworkers are really busy as well. So, you simply accept extreme busyness as the norm.

Your limiting belief is that there isn't enough time in the day to get things done.

But does this have to be the norm? It doesn't.

Rewriting The Limiting Belief

Let's transform the *limiting* belief that there isn't enough time into an *empowering* belief.

Limiting Belief:

- "I don't have enough time."

Empowering Beliefs:

- "I have time for my most important tasks."
- "My schedule gives me freedom from time pressure."
- "I refuse to let time rule my life."
- "I get things done without worrying about time."
- "I am productive and make the best out of the time I have been given."

The best way to make these newfound empowering beliefs work for you is to work on the thing that matters to you most FIRST thing in the day.

By making quick progress on the tasks that matter most, you'll feel more productive. You'll slash the limiting belief.

This principle is often called "Slaying your dragons."

In other words, you "slay" your most important task, your "dragon," first thing in the morning. Before you get started on the thousand other tasks that vie for your attention, give your full focus to the one thing that matters the most to you. To the thing that will move your forward the most.

By doing your most important thing first, you rewrite your limiting belief that there is not enough time in the day to work on what matters. Your new belief becomes: "There is plenty of time to do what matters because I work on what matters first."

Action Steps

- Write down all the tasks you need to perform in a given day.
- Organize those tasks by importance.
- Determine your *most* important task for the day.
- Give all your attention to working on that task until it's done.
- Repeat this process each day.

Affirmation

There is more than enough time in each day for me to accomplish the tasks that matter most. I am dedicated to and focused on getting the most important things done each day.

I refuse to be easily distracted. Rather, I slay my dragons first thing each morning. I do less important things later, after I finish the task that matters most.

I am passionate about getting things done that are important to me.

Looking Forward

In the next chapter, you'll learn that you're never too old to start a new project or begin working toward a new goal. Yes, you can teach an old dog new tricks, and the next lesson shows you how.

Self-Reflection Questions

Does extreme busyness have to be the norm?

Is it true that there's not enough time in the day to get everything done?

What does it mean to "slay your dragons"?

Why is it so important to focus on your most important tasks first?

How does focusing on your most important tasks first free you up to achieve more during the day?

CHAPTER 29

Limiting Belief #2: I'm Too Old To Start Something New

Story – Sarah
Genesis 21:1-6
¹"The Lord kept His word and did for Sarah exactly what He had promised. ²She became pregnant [in her old age] and she gave birth to a son for Abraham in his old age [100 years old]." (New Living Translation)

In the last chapter, you learned how to be more productive. In this chapter, you can carry your new techniques with you as you see how age doesn't limit you either.

With this self-limiting belief, you believe that in order to be successful, you need to start young. That the only way to truly achieve great things is to get started at a young age and work and work until you finally achieve greatness at an older age. That you're too old to start new things, reset your career, start a new hobby, or strive after new goals.

Your limiting belief is that you can't teach an old dog new tricks.

You feel like if you tried to start something new at this

point in your life, you would fail. Maybe you want to write a book. Maybe you want to take up skiing. Maybe you want to completely change your career. Maybe you want to run a marathon.

But as you consider these things, you think to yourself, *"Only young people do these things. I'm simply too old to get started on something this big."*

But this limiting belief simply isn't true. It needs to be rewritten.

Rewriting The Limiting Belief

Now let's rewrite this limiting belief into an empowering belief.

Limiting Belief:

- "I'm too old to accomplish anything new."

Empowering Beliefs:

- "My age gives me wisdom."
- "I have more experience than those who are younger."
- "I can avoid mistakes that younger people make."
- "My experience will allow me to get going faster."
- "I'm never too old to start something new."

There are thousands of people who have achieved huge amounts of success later in life.

Joy Behar, former host of *The View*, didn't start her career in show business until she was 40. Vera Wang didn't start designing clothing until she was 40. Harland Sanders, the founder of Kentucky Fried Chicken, was broke until he finally found success at age 65. Charles Darwin published his most famous book, *The Origin of Species*, at age 50.

If they can do it, surely you can too. In order to rewrite your limiting belief, you need to realize that being older gives you more wisdom. You have more to offer, a broader skill set, and more experience. This actually gives you a distinct advantage over those who are younger.

Younger people are prone to make more mistakes because they don't have the experience that you have. This keeps them from achieving success as quickly as they might. Because you have so much experience and wisdom, you are able to achieve success more quickly because you can avoid mistakes.

Your new belief is: "I can start something new at any age. I have the experience and wisdom to achieve anything I want, regardless of my age."

Action Steps

- Write down all the things you want to achieve.
- Write down the distinct advantages you have because you're older. Include your experiences and the lessons you've learned through those experiences.
- Think back on all the things you've already achieved in your life and let these encourage you as you attempt new things.
- Affirm each day that you are enough and that you can achieve whatever you set your mind to.
- Read inspirational stories of others who have achieved great things at an older age.

Affirmation

I can start something new at any age. In fact, my age gives me a distinct advantage over those who are younger. I relish the experience and wisdom that age has provided me.

I am confident that I can achieve whatever I put my mind to. I refuse to believe the lie that my age limits me.

As I look back on my life, I see all the things I've already achieved, and this gives me great confidence that I can achieve new things as well.

Looking Forward

Now that you see how to keep time and age from stopping you, you'll be excited to discover in the next chapter how failures actually bring you closer to your goals!

Self-Reflection Questions

Why do we often feel like we're too old to start something new?

How does age actually benefit you when it comes to starting new things?

How old is too old when it comes to trying new things?

How does the example of others inspire you to try new things at an older age?

CHAPTER 30

Limiting Belief #3: Past Failure Means Future Failure

Story – Hagar
Genesis 21:8-20
[13]" But I will also make a nation of the descendants of Hagar's son because he is your son, too." (New Living Translation)

In previous chapters you discovered how time and age don't have to limit you at all! Another belief that limits many people is, "Once a failure, always a failure." Let's put that belief out of its misery right now.

If you've ever tried and failed at something in the past, it's easy to assume that your past failure means that you'll fail again in the future. That past outcomes guarantee future outcomes. That you're always doomed to fail at whatever you attempt.

You may be tempted to think, *"I always fail at this so why should this time be any different? I'm just a failure overall."*

Your limiting belief is that your past failure means future failure. You assume that the past governs the future. That if something didn't work in previous attempts, it won't work in the future.

Rewriting The Limiting Belief

Now let's rewrite this limiting belief into empowering beliefs.

Limiting Belief:

- "Past failure means future failure."

Empowering Beliefs:

- "My past failures have no bearing on my future."
- "Past failures help me avoid future mistakes."
- "I've simply discovered a way that doesn't work."
- "Each failure brings me one step closer to success."

The simple truth is that your past failures do not have any bearing on your current endeavors. Just because you've failed in the past doesn't mean that you'll fail in the future.

In fact, failure in the past is actually an advantage! You've discovered one way that doesn't work, which means you can avoid that way moving forward.

Thomas Edison struggled for years to figure out how to invent a functioning lightbulb. When asked how he kept going in spite of so much "failure," he said, "I have not failed. I've just found 10,000 ways that won't work."

It's important to adopt a similar belief. You haven't failed in the past. You've simply discovered one particular way that doesn't work. This has gotten you one step closer to your success.

Or consider the wise words of Winston Churchill: "Success consists of going from failure to failure without loss of enthusiasm."

If you want to succeed, it's crucial to understand that failure in the past doesn't have any bearing on your future. Every "failure" brings you one step closer to the success you desire.

Action Steps

- Write down the ways you think you have "failed" in the past.
- Determine how each failure has actually brought you closer to success.
- Resolve that you will not let past failures keep you from pursuing what really matters to you.

Affirmation

I avoid thinking that my past failures could ever cause me to fail now or in the future. I affirm that each past failure has actually brought me one step closer to success. I am closer to success now than I ever have been in the past.

I refuse to let my past failures keep me from pursuing what really matters to me.

I am committed to my success, regardless of the past.

Looking Forward

In the next chapter, you'll discover how you can learn from your past and look forward to a bright future.

Self-Reflection Questions

Why do we assume that failure in the past means failure in the future?

Does failure in the past *really* mean that you'll fail in the future?

How do your past experiences (and even failures) actually help you be more successful in the future?

What lessons can you learn from your past failures that will help you succeed in the future?

CHAPTER 31

Limiting Belief #4: My Past Will Always Negatively Influence My Future

Story – Rahab
Joshua 2:1-24
"It was by faith that Rahab the prostitute was not destroyed with the people in her city who refused to obey God. For she had given a friendly welcome to the spies." Hebrews 11:31
(New Living Translation)

In the previous chapter, you discovered how your failures don't keep you from succeeding now. In fact, failures bring you closer to success! This lesson is tied closely to the same concept – that what happened in your past doesn't predict your future.

If you think that your past does predict your future, this limiting belief is particularly pernicious. It's the assumption that past events will influence future events in a negative way. That your past actions hold too much sway over your future actions.

Maybe you've made mistakes in the past and you're convinced that they're going to keep you from achieving the success you desire. Maybe you've tried things in the past that simply haven't worked. Maybe you don't have a good track record in a particular area.

Your limiting belief is that your past holds sway over your future.

You believe that your past actions restrict your future options, or that your past efforts will hamper your future efforts.

And so, you don't feel like you can try anything new. You feel like your past is holding you back. Keeping you from your true potential. Standing in the way of your success.

Rewriting The Limiting Belief

Let's rewrite the limiting belief into a set of empowering beliefs.

Limiting Belief:

- "My past will always keep me from creating a bright future."

Empowering Beliefs:

- "My past can't determine what I achieve in the future."
- "My past is one of my greatest assets."
- "Lessons from the past make me wiser."
- "I can avoid mistakes in the future by looking to the past."
- "I can learn from my past and adapt and change."

In order to rewrite this limiting belief, it's crucial to understand that your past actions have no bearing on your future. This is not to say that the past doesn't matter. But your past cannot determine what you do or don't achieve in the future.

Failure in the past doesn't automatically mean failure in the future. Struggle in the past doesn't automatically mean struggle in the future.

In fact, your past is one of your greatest assets. As you learn lessons from the past, it makes you that much wiser. You have more knowledge, skills, and experience. You can avoid the mistakes of the past and succeed that much faster in the future.

In some ways, it is true that the past influences the future, but it can always influence the future in good ways! Your past allows you to adapt, change, and become more effective at what you do.

Action Steps

- Identify any areas of your past that you feel will negatively influence your future.
- Ask yourself, "How will these elements of my past actually *help* me as I move forward into the future?"
- Write down every advantage that your past gives you.

Affirmation

I affirm that my past fails to determine my future. In fact, it gives me great advantages. I alone determine my future.

I adapt, change, and evolve in positive ways because of my past. I am becoming a wiser person because of my past and I know that the future holds many good things for me.

I can achieve great things because I am wiser and more skilled than in the past. My past has taught me valuable lessons. I am grateful for these lessons and ready to move on toward the bright future that awaits me.

Looking Forward

In the next chapter, you'll be happy to learn that you have everything you need to achieve your biggest dreams and goals!

Self-Reflection Questions

Why is it so easy to believe that the past will negatively influence the future?

Does your past actually affect your future? How?

In what ways is your past one of your greatest assets?

How does your past influence the future in *good* ways?

CHAPTER 32

Limiting Belief #5: My Resources Are Limited

Story – The Prophet's Widow
2 Kings 4:1-7
[7]"When she told the man of God what had happened, he said to her, "Now sell the olive oil and pay your debts, and you and your sons can live on what is left over." (New Living Translation)

In the previous chapter, you conquered the limiting belief that your past controls your future. This chapter steps even farther out of your past and looks at your current circumstances. Do you feel like your resources are limited?

If so, this mentality assumes that there are only a limited number of resources and options in the world. It operates out of what is called a "scarcity" mentality, which is the belief that there are only so many resources in the world and that most of these resources have been taken by others.

This leads you to assume that there aren't enough resources for you to do what you want to do.

You think to yourself, *"I don't have enough [time, money, connections, etc.] to achieve what I want to achieve."*

Because you assume that you don't have enough resources and options, you fail to take action. Instead of moving forward, you spin your wheels. You think that in order to take action, you need to have more options at your disposal, such as more time, money, or help from others.

Rewriting The Limiting Belief

Now let's rewrite the limiting belief with a set of empowering beliefs.

Limiting Belief:

- "I don't have enough resources."

Empowering Beliefs:

- "The universe is full of abundant resources."
- "There is more than enough to go around."
- "I can get whatever I need to accomplish my wildest dreams."
- "The universe has my back."
- "I create more of what I focus on."

The reality is that we live in an abundant universe that has more than enough for everyone. There is no limit to the resources available if you simply start looking for them and opening yourself to receive them.

This mindset is called an "abundance" mindset. Instead of believing that there are very few resources available, you believe that there is more than enough to go around. You can get whatever you need to accomplish your dreams. Instead of dreaming small and limited dreams, you dream big because you know that all that you need is available.

Your new belief is that the universe has everything you need in order to achieve your biggest dreams and goals.

You simply need to be open to all that the universe has to offer you. Focus on the abundance that you want to receive. After all, we create more of what we focus on.

If you want to receive more from the universe, focus on what you want to receive and believe that you'll get it. Faith is the key. You must believe that the universe has your back.

Action Steps

- Daily repeat the affirmation, "The universe has my back and gives me everything I need to achieve my goals and dreams."
- Make a list of all the specific things you need to receive in order achieve your biggest hopes and dreams.
- Instead of focusing on what you don't have, fix all your attention on what you want to receive. You create more of what you focus on.

Affirmation

The universe is abundant and has my back in every way. I believe there is more than enough for me and that resources are plentiful.

Everything I need to achieve my goals comes my way

when I need them, and I gratefully and wholeheartedly open myself up to receive them.

I dream big, abundant dreams, knowing that big, abundant things are coming my way. With eager expectation, I look forward to the future, knowing that it is good and exciting.

Looking Forward

Since resources aren't an issue, you may wonder if you're now expected to make big strides toward your goals. Luckily, success doesn't depend on big wins. You'll discover in the next chapter how small successes add up to big progress.

Self-Reflection Questions

What is a "scarcity" mindset?

How does a scarcity mindset keep your from taking action?

What is an abundance mindset?

Why is it so important to focus on abundance rather than scarcity?

Do you believe the universe "has your back"? Why?

CHAPTER 33

Limiting Belief #6: Lack Of Major Progress Means Failure

Story – Rizpah
2 Samuel 21:1-14
10"Then Rizpah daughter of Aiah, the mother of two of the men, spread burlap on a rock and stayed there the entire harvest season. She prevented the scavenger birds from tearing at their bodies during the day and stopped wild animals from eating them at night." (New Living Translation)

In the last chapter, you learned that all the resources you need to reach your goals are available to you. Today, you'll discover that you don't need big wins to reach your goals – small successes get you there as well.

Oh, how easy it is to criticize yourself for a lack of major progress on your goals. You feel that if you're not making significant progress every single day, then you're a failure. Maybe you have a list of goals that you want to achieve and that list haunts you. It's a reminder of all that you haven't achieved.

Each day you feel like a failure. You feel like truly productive people make leaps and bounds of progress on a consistent basis.

Your limiting belief is that lack of major progress on your goals means that you're a failure.

You constantly criticize and berate yourself for not achieving more. For not being more successful. For not accomplishing more - faster. There are times when you're really frustrated with yourself and feel like giving up altogether.

Rewriting The Limiting Belief

Now let's rewrite this limiting belief into a set of empowering beliefs.

Limiting Belief:

- "Lack of major progress means failure."

Empowering Beliefs:

- "Small progress equals a big win."
- "Small successes add up to big progress over time."
- "I celebrate my victories no matter what size they are."
- "Consistency is what matters most."

In order to rewrite this belief, you must understand that even the smallest progress on your goals is a big win. Small bits of progress on a consistent basis add up over time to big successes. You may not be making huge amounts of progress on a daily basis, *and that's OKAY.*

Your new belief becomes: "Any progress is a win."

Did you take one small step toward your goal? That's a

win! Even if you only do one thing per day or per week toward your goals, that's progress and should be celebrated.

Avoid judging your success by whether you're making big jumps forward. Judge your success by your consistency.

And if you're having trouble being consistent with your goals, that's okay. Go back to the action steps for limiting belief number one. Focus on your most important task first thing each day and seek to just make a small amount of progress on your task.

Action Steps

- Break down your big goals into very small, manageable pieces.
- Each day seek to get one small element of your goal done.
- Instead of evaluating how much progress you're making on your goals, trust the process of doing one small thing every single day.

Affirmation

I affirm that I AM making progress on my goals, even if that progress may seem small and relatively insignificant.

I choose to celebrate my small wins, knowing that each small win brings me one step closer to my overall goal.

I refuse to criticize myself for what I perceive to be a lack of progress. Instead, I focus all my attention on the small steps forward I am taking because each small step forward is a victory.

Looking Forward

The next chapter tackles a trap that many of us fall into – comparing yourself to others. You'll see how this habit robs you of joy while destroying your confidence. Luckily, you'll discover tools to help you break out of this need and realize how valuable you really are.

Self-Reflection Questions

Do you criticize yourself for not being more productive? Why?

Why is it so important to celebrate small wins?

Why is consistency more important than making big jumps forward?

What small steps can you take this week to make progress on your goals?

CHAPTER 34

Limiting Belief #7: I Compare Myself To Others

Story – Hannah
1 Samuel 1:1—2:11
⁶"So Peninnah would taunt Hanna and make fun of her because the Lord had kept her from having children. ⁷Year after year it was the same—Peninnah would taunt Hannah as they went to the Tabernacle. Each time, Hannah would be reduced to tears and would not eat."

Previously, you looked at how criticizing yourself for your lack of great progress could make you feel like giving up altogether.

Today, you'll discover how comparing yourself to others can make you feel the same way. Of course, we'll give you the tools to crush this limiting belief. Let's see how...

It's incredibly easy and common to compare yourself to others. You look at the success someone else is having and then compare that to your own levels of success. You compare your accomplishments to the accomplishments of others. You judge yourself by what others are achieving.

If someone else seems to be accomplishing more than you, it makes you feel like a failure.

You feel like you should be accomplishing at least as much, if not more, than others. And so, you feel terrible about yourself. As if you don't have much to offer the world. Even like a loser, of sorts.

Theodore Roosevelt famously said, "Comparison is the thief of joy." So, when you compare yourself to others, you allow their achievements to determine how much joy you experience.

Rewriting The Limiting Belief

Now let's rewrite this limiting belief into a set of empowering beliefs.

Limiting Belief:

- "I compare myself to others."

Empowering Beliefs:

- "The achievements of others don't determine my value."
- "I am valuable simply because of who I am."
- "I refuse to compare myself to others."
- "What matters most is what I achieve, not what others achieve."
- "I am more than my accomplishments."

In order for you to rewrite this limiting belief in your mind, it's essential to understand that the achievements of others simply don't matter for you. It's not that they aren't important. But they don't determine your worth, success, or value.

You are valuable simply because of who you are. You are inherently valuable and worthy. Your successes should be celebrated, not compared to the successes of others.

It doesn't matter how much someone else succeeds. What matters is what you achieve.

Your new belief is, "I am worthy, and I refuse to compare myself to others. Whether I achieve 'a lot' or 'a little,' I am still valuable and worthy."

In our performance-driven culture, it's easy to believe that we're nothing more than our accomplishments. But nothing could be further from the truth. Our value simply comes from who we are as people.

Yes, it's important to be productive and seek to accomplish our goals. But if we're constantly comparing ourselves to others, we'll never be happy. As Theodore Roosevelt said, our joy will be stolen by comparing ourselves to others.

Action Steps

- Regularly remind yourself that your value is not tied to your achievements.
- Daily affirm that you are enough and that you are worthy.
- Refuse to compare yourself to others.

Affirmation

I refuse to believe that my value is tied to my achieve-

ments. I know that I am valuable and worthy simply because of who I am.

Whether I achieve "a lot" or "a little," I know that I am still enough, and I refuse to compare myself to others. The achievements of others have no bearing on my value.

I celebrate my successes without worrying about the accomplishments of others.

I. Am. Enough.

Looking Forward

In the next chapter, you'll discover why you WANT to take responsibility for your own circumstances.

Self-Reflection Questions

Do you often compare yourself to others? Why is this so unhelpful?

What does it mean that, "Comparison is the thief of joy"?

Do the achievements of others affect your value or worth?

Why is it so important to understand that you are more valuable than your accomplishments?

How does comparing yourself to others keep you from being happy?

CHAPTER 35

Limiting Belief #8: I Am Not Responsible For My Current Situation

Story – Eve
Genesis 3:1-24
⁶"The woman was convinced. She saw that the tree was beautiful, and its fruit looked delicious, and she wanted the wisdom it would give her. So, she took some of the fruit and ate it. Then she gave some to her husband, who was with her, and he ate it, too." (New Living Translation)

Congratulations! You've made it half-way through! You've tackled some major self-limiting beliefs and may already be seeing light at the end of the tunnel.

Now, we'll analyze how harmful it is when you think that you're just a victim of circumstances. This belief severely limits you. Let's see how...

It's easy to play the blame game. To believe that someone else is responsible for the situation you find yourself currently in. To assume that your circumstances are the products of other people's actions.

When you don't hold yourself responsible for your current circumstances, it allows you to stay stuck in those circumstances. After all, if you didn't create the circumstances, surely you can't be responsible for changing them.

And so, you don't make any forward progress. You think things like, *"I can't believe that they put me in this position. This is not my fault. I am not responsible for where I currently am."*

Your limiting belief is that you are not responsible for where you currently are in life.

This limiting belief allows you to play the victim. When something goes wrong, you can simply blame it on others and the circumstances they've put you in. You refuse to take ownership of your situation.

Rewriting The Limiting Belief

Now let's rewrite this limiting belief into a set of empowering beliefs.

Limiting Belief:

- "I'm not responsible for where I am in life."

Empowering Beliefs:

- "I am 100% responsible for my life."
- "I take ownership of all my circumstances."
- "I refuse to play the victim game."
- "I can create whatever circumstances I want."
- "I am in complete charge of my life and determine what it looks like."

If you're going to make forward progress in life, it's absolutely essential that you take 100% responsibility for the circumstances in which you find yourself. Yes, other people play a role in your life, but ultimately, you are responsible for what you accept and what you refuse.

If you find yourself in a particular set of circumstances, it's because you've accepted them. You've decided that you were okay with those circumstances and haven't made any significant efforts to change them.

Your new belief is: "I am 100% responsible for every area of my life."

This is actually an incredibly freeing belief. Once you realize that you created your current circumstances, you can then go about changing them.

You can take the actions necessary to change your life in incredible, amazing ways. You don't have to stay stuck. You don't have to play the victim. You are in charge of your life, and you can shape your life to be however you want it to be.

Action Steps

- Write down any circumstances you are unhappy about.
- Take 100% ownership of those circumstances, even if others played a part in creating them.
- Identify specific action steps you must take to change your circumstances.
- Daily affirm that you are completely in control of your life and that you are 100% responsible for all the outcomes.

Affirmation

I am the captain of my fate. I am responsible for everything positive and negative that comes into my life.

I take 100% ownership for the current state of my life. I do what is necessary to create the life I desire.

I refuse to play the victim of circumstances beyond my control or feel that I am at the mercy of others. Instead, I take action. This is my life and I can build it how I please.

Looking Forward

Perhaps success has eluded you because you feel that you aren't worthy of success. This belief could very well be working on a subconscious level, keeping you from ever reaching your goals. Discover how to overcome this belief in the next chapter.

Self-Reflection Questions

Why is it so important to accept 100% responsibility for your circumstances?

What happens when you refuse to take ownership of your current circumstances?

Do you believe that you are 100% responsible for everything that happens in your life?

Why is it freeing to start taking total ownership for every circumstance in your life?

CHAPTER 36

Limiting Belief #9: I Don't Deserve Success

Story – The Canaanite Woman
Mark 7:24-30
28"She replied, "That's true, Lord but even the dogs under the table are allowed to eat the scraps from the children's plates." (New Living Translation)

In the last chapter, you learned how taking responsibility for your circumstances actually provides you a way out of them. But what if – even if you do take responsibility – you never seem to achieve your goals? In this lesson, you'll discover a possible cause and learn how to overcome it.

With this self-limiting belief, regardless of how much progress you make, you always fall short.

It could be that deep down, for whatever reason, you don't believe that you deserve success. You feel that you're not good enough, smart enough, or lovable enough to be worthy of success.

This is a very devious, insidious limiting belief.

You believe that others are worthy of success, but when you look at your own life, you refuse to believe that you should experience it.

This can lead you to self-sabotage. When you start to get close to success, you begin to do things that limit you. Maybe you're even afraid of succeeding, and so the closer you get to success, the more scared you get.

Your limiting belief is that you are unworthy of success.

This seriously limits the progress you can make. After all, you can't achieve big things if you don't think that you deserve them. You won't have the motivation to keep going if you feel unworthy of success.

You absolutely must rewrite this belief.

Rewriting The Belief

Now let's rewrite this limiting belief with a set of empowering beliefs.

Limiting Belief:

- "I am unworthy of success."

Empowering Beliefs:

- "I am inherently worthy of success."
- "I am valuable simply because of who I am."
- "I deserve success and all the benefits that come with it."

Ask yourself this question: Who is worthy of success?

The answer is EVERYONE, including you. There is no reason that you shouldn't experience success.

Remember, you are worthy and valuable simply because of who you are. You don't have to do anything to make yourself worthy of success. You are worthy of succeeding simply because you are you.

Your new belief becomes, "I am worthy of all the success in the world."

No matter what anyone has told you, you deserve success and all the benefits that come with it. You deserve to achieve big things and make your dreams come true. If you work hard, you are worthy of the reward that you receive in return.

Action Steps

- Write down every reason you think that you are *not* worthy of success.
- Cross out all those reasons.
- Replace that list with a list of reasons you truly *are* worthy of success.
- Review that list on a daily basis.

Affirmation

I affirm that I am worthy of all the success in the world.

Regardless of what anyone has said to me, regardless of what I have thought in the past, I choose now to believe that I am worthy of success.

I believe that I deserve to achieve all my biggest dreams and accomplish my most worthy goals. I refuse to think small, unworthy thoughts about myself. Instead, I embrace my greatness, knowing that I am worthy simply because of who I am.

Looking Forward

Do you worry about what others think about you? Are you afraid to pursue your goals because of what someone else thinks about it? In the next chapter, you'll discover how your own opinion of yourself is the only one that matters.

Self-Reflection Questions

What are some of the reasons people don't believe that they are worthy of success?

Why does not believing you're worthy of success often lead to self-sabotage?

Who is worthy of success?

Why are you worthy of success?

CHAPTER 37

Limiting Belief #10: I Worry What Others Think About Me

Story – Adulteress
John 8:1-11
[7]"They kept demanding an answer, so he stood up again and said, "All right, but let the one who has never sinned throw the first stone!"
(New Living Translation)

In the last chapter, you learned how to instill the positive belief that you're worthy of success.

Do you still doubt? Do you wonder what others think about you? Today, we'll look at this limiting belief.

This is one of the most common limiting beliefs that people struggle with. You worry, and even obsess over, what others think about you.

You worry that if you're too successful, people will think you're stuck up. You worry that if you're not successful enough, people will look down on you.

If you stand up for yourself, you worry that people will

think you're too assertive. If you try to be a peacemaker, you worry that you'll come across as a doormat.

Worrying about what others think of you can be incredibly consuming. It can sap your time, energy, and joy. It keeps you from being productive and often causes you to second guess yourself.

Your limiting belief is that if you do (or don't do) certain actions, others will think less of you.

If this limiting belief is not kept in check, it can become an obsession. It can keep you from pursuing your dreams and cause you to constantly be afraid of what others are thinking.

The fear of what others think can be like a great weight hanging around your neck, dragging you down, keeping you from making forward progress.

Rewriting Your Limiting Belief

Now let's rewrite this limiting belief with a set of empowering beliefs.

Limiting Belief:

- "I worry about what others will think about me."

Empowering Beliefs:

- "What others think of me doesn't matter."
- "What truly matters is what I think of myself."
- "My opinion of myself is the one that counts."
- "I am secure in who I am."
- "I avoid striving to make everyone happy."

The key to rewriting this limiting belief is to realize that what others think of you simply doesn't matter. In the long scheme of things, does it matter if others think more or less of you? No, it doesn't.

What truly matters is what you think of yourself.

Your opinion of yourself is the one that counts the most. And as we've said before, you are worthy and valuable. That's the opinion you should have of yourself. Don't let the opinions of others drag you down. Their opinions hold no weight compared to your own opinion of yourself.

Your new belief is that the opinions of others don't affect you one way or the other.

You are free from caring what others think of you. You are secure in yourself, knowing that you are valuable and worthy. You no longer strive to make everyone happy. Rather, you focus on making yourself happy and ensuring that you're pursuing your dreams and goals.

Action Steps

- Regularly look in the mirror and say to yourself, "I don't have to make everyone else happy. My opinion of myself is all that matters."
- Create a list that says, "People I Must Please" at the top. Leave the list blank as a statement that you're done with worrying about what others think about you.

Affirmation

I refuse to play the people-pleasing game. I affirm that the opinions of others fail to have any sway over me. My opinion of myself is all that matters.

I strive to achieve my dreams and accomplish my goals without worrying what others think about me.

I choose to believe the best about myself at all times. I avoid letting the opinions of others drag me down or pull me off course.

Looking Forward

Now that you've learned to ignore what others think, let's look at how you treat yourself. You act kindly toward others – how kind are you to yourself? In the next chapter, you'll learn how such kindness can help you reach your goals faster and easier.

Self-Reflection Questions

What are some of the negative effects of constantly worrying what others think about you?

How does fear of what others think keep you from pursuing your dreams?

Do the opinions of others about you truly matter?

What are some of the benefits of not caring what others may think about you?

CHAPTER 38

Limiting Belief #11: I Don't Give Myself The Love, Compassion, and Understanding I Give To Others

Story – Tamar
Genesis 38
[26]"Judah recognized them immediately and said, "She [Tamar] is more righteous than I am, because I didn't arrange for her to marry my son Shelah." And Judah never slept with Tamar again."

In the last chapter, you learned that your opinion of yourself is the only one that matters. In this lesson, you'll see that how you treat yourself matters, too.

You are a compassionate, kind, and loving person. When someone makes a mistake, you are gracious toward them, understanding that everyone makes mistakes.

You are patient with others, giving them time to learn and change. If someone struggles with a particular task or doesn't make as much progress on a task as expected, you give them grace.

But you don't treat yourself in the same way.

For some reason, you don't believe that you deserve the same love, compassion, grace, and understanding that you give to others.

Maybe you were told from a young age that you needed to be perfect. Maybe you've somehow unconsciously adopted the idea that you shouldn't make the same mistakes that others make.

Whatever the case, you are really hard on yourself.

Your limiting belief is that you should be perfect, and if you're not perfect you feel like you need to punish yourself.

When you make a mistake, you endlessly berate yourself, feeling like you shouldn't have made it. You're not compassionate and gracious toward yourself. You don't love yourself very much. You hold yourself to an impossible standard.

This limiting belief makes you feel like you're never enough. Like you're never worthy, never acceptable, never doing enough things. It's a very unhappy limiting belief.

Rewriting The Limiting Belief

Now let's rewrite the limiting belief with a set of empowering beliefs.

Limiting Belief:

- "I don't give myself the love, compassion, and understanding I give to others."

Empowering Belief:

- "I'm human and it's okay to make mistakes."
- "I deserve the same grace, compassion, and understanding that I give to others."
- "I am patient and loving toward myself."
- "I treat myself the same way that I treat others."

It's really important to rewrite this limiting belief. If you don't, you'll always be unhappy, miserable, and feel like you're never doing enough.

Please understand that, just like everyone else, you are human. You make mistakes, and that's okay. You have off days, and that's not a problem. There are times when you're not as productive or don't get as much done, and there's nothing wrong with that.

In other words, you're not perfect (and you're not supposed to be).

Your new belief is that you deserve the same grace, compassion, love, and patience that you extend to others.

You are patient with others. Be patient with yourself. You are loving toward others. Be loving toward yourself. You have compassion and mercy for others, so have compassion and mercy for yourself.

Simply put, avoid being so hard on yourself! You're human, and humans aren't perfect. You deserve kind treatment from yourself.

Action Steps

- The next time you're being hard on yourself, ask yourself this question: *"How would I treat someone else who is in my shoes?"*
- Extend that same loving, gracious treatment to-

ward yourself. Apply the Golden Rule to yourself. Get into a habit of treating yourself just like anybody else.

Affirmation

I am human, just like everyone else. It is okay for me to struggle and make mistakes. When that happens, I deserve the same compassion and grace that I give to others.

I refuse to hold myself to a standard that I avoid holding others to. I love myself, even when things turn out imperfectly.

I treat myself as I treat others - with love, compassion, and patience.

Looking Forward

Do you feel that asking for help makes you look weak? In the next chapter, you'll discover that it's actually a strength. Learn the benefits of working with others and how to make this a belief that helps – not hinders – you.

Self-Reflection Questions

Why is it often easier to be compassionate and loving toward others rather than yourself?

Why do you believe that you're not worthy of love, compassion, grace, and understanding?

What are some of the negative effects of feeling like you're never doing enough?

Why is it so important to allow yourself to not be perfect?

What are some ways you can be loving and understanding toward yourself today?

CHAPTER 39

Limiting Belief #12: I Can Do Everything Myself

Story – Hemorrhaging Woman
Luke 8:43-48
44"Coming up behind Jesus, she touched the fringe of his robe. Immediately, the bleeding stopped." (New Living Translation)

In the last chapter, you learned how treating yourself with kindness helps you reach your goals. Today, you'll discover how letting others help you can benefit you in many ways.

In our culture, it's extremely easy to feel like you need to do everything yourself. To feel like you can't ask for help. To feel like asking for help is a sign of weakness. And if you're especially competent, maybe you can do many things without the help of others.

And so, you never ask for assistance. You try to do everything on your own, thinking that if you can get by without the help of others, that it's a sign of strength.

But in reality, not being able to ask for help is a sign of weakness. The truth is that none of us can do everything on our own. We all have limitations, blind spots, and areas of weakness. None of us are perfect or able to accomplish all things on our own.

Your limiting belief is that you can do everything yourself without any help.

We inherently need other people, and your inability to ask for help actually keeps you from accomplishing as much as you could. If you teamed up with others, your combined strengths would allow you to achieve far more than you could on your own.

Rewriting Your Limiting Belief

Now let's rewrite this limiting belief with a set of empowering beliefs.

Limiting Belief:

- "I can do everything without help."

Empowering Beliefs:

- "I can benefit from the help and assistance of others."
- "Others have strengths and talents that I don't have."
- "I can better reach my full potential with the help of others."
- "I can't do everything by myself."

In order to rewrite this limiting belief, you must come to terms with the fact that you simply can't do *everything*.

Yes, you may be able to accomplish a lot. But the simple truth is that others have strengths and gifts that you don't have, and you can tap into those strengths and gifts. You need to utilize the abilities of others.

The more you tap into the strengths of others, the more you'll be able to get done and the closer you'll come to actually achieving your goals, hopes, and dreams. If you try to do everything alone, you simply won't get as far.

Your new belief is that you need the help of others in order to reach your true potential.

Don't try to be a Lone Ranger. You have so much potential, but you need others to help you fully realize it. Ask for help. Utilize the gifts and talents that others have. You'll make so much more progress than if you try to do everything by yourself.

Action Steps

- Write down the names of five people whom you work closely with.
- For each person, write down their unique strengths.
- Seek out at least one person on your list to help you with a current project or task.

Affirmation

Although I am skilled, talented, and capable, I affirm that I need the help and assistance of others. They supplement my talents so that, together, we can excel at any task and even get the job done quicker than I could on my own.

I seek out others to help me at each step of my journey. I avoid trying to do everything myself. Rather, I depend on other people to help me reach my full potential.

Looking Forward

Do you sometimes feel that you got the short end of the stick when they handed out intelligence? Is it hard for you to learn new things? This belief limits you. In the next chapter, you'll see how to turn that belief into this belief instead: "I have an incredible ability to learn."

Self-Reflection Questions

Why might you be tempted to think you can do everything on your own?

Is it a sign of weakness when you ask for help? Why or why not?

What are some of the reasons you need other people?

How can you benefit from the gifts and strengths of others?

Why do you need others in order to reach your true potential?

CHAPTER 40

Limiting Belief #13: I'm Not Smart Enough

Story – Rhoda
Acts 12:1-19
[15]*"You're out of your mind!" they [the Disciples] said. When she [the servant girl named Rhoda] insisted, they decided, "It must be an angel."*
(New Living Translation)

In the previous chapter, you learned how to let others help you reach your goals faster and easier. But even with the help of others, you could be severely limiting yourself if you think that you're not smart enough.

This self-limiting belief has the potential to keep you from trying many new things. You feel like you're not smart enough to achieve a particular task or goal. Like you don't have the necessary intelligence to accomplish what you truly want to accomplish. Like you're lacking the needed knowledge to get something done.

Maybe this belief was instilled in you from a young age by an unkind adult. Maybe you struggled with particular tasks in school which made you assume that you just weren't a smart person. Or maybe you heard your parents say this about themselves.

Your limiting belief is that you aren't smart enough to do what you really want to do.

This belief can keep you from even trying to do new things. You can feel so intimidated at the thought of trying to learn something new that you won't even start. You feel like your supposed lack of knowledge is a handicap and that if you were only smarter you could do what you wanted.

Rewriting The Limiting Belief

Now let's rewrite this limiting belief with a set of empowering beliefs.

Limiting belief:

- "I'm not smart enough."

Empowering Belief:

- "I've accomplished so much already in my life."
- "If I wasn't smart, I wouldn't have gotten this far in life."
- "I have an incredible ability to learn."
- "I can do anything I set my mind to."

This limiting belief is false on so many levels. First and foremost, you truly are much smarter than you realize.

Think of all you've already accomplished in your life. If you weren't smart, you wouldn't have been able to achieve all that you have. Your past successes prove that you're smarter than you think you are.

Second, you have an incredible ability to learn. Consider all the things you've learned to do over the course of your life. Your brain is a sponge, and you're able to learn almost anything you set your mind to. Even if you don't have the knowledge to accomplish a particular task, that doesn't mean you can't learn it.

Your new belief is that you are incredibly smart and are able to learn anything you set your mind to.

This changes the way you approach new tasks. Instead of fearing having to learn things, you eagerly anticipate the challenge. Instead of doubting yourself, you're confident in your ability to tackle any task. You know that you're very smart and that no task is too complicated for you to learn.

Action Steps

- Make a big list of things that you've accomplished in your life. Include little things, such as learning to ride a bike, and bigger things, such as learning your current job.
- Any time you're tempted to doubt your intelligence, go back to that list to remind yourself of how smart you really are and that you have the ability to learn anything you set your mind to.

Affirmation

I am highly intelligent and accomplished. I have already achieved many things in my life, which proves my intelligence.

Whenever I need a clearer understanding of something,

I am able to quickly learn it, grasping all the nuances of the subject.

I refuse to doubt my intelligence. I know that I am smart enough. I embrace the fact that I am naturally smart and able to accomplish anything I set my mind to.

Looking Forward

Now that you've conquered many beliefs that limit you, it's time to get started moving toward your goals with excitement and confidence. But wait – what if a self-limiting belief keeps you from getting started in the first place? No worries! We'll get you moving in the next chapter.

Self-Reflection Questions

What are some reasons you may feel like you're not smart enough to achieve your goals?

How does feeling not smart enough keep you from making forward progress?

What are some of the things you've accomplished in your life? How do these things prove your intelligence?

What are some things you've learned over the course of your life? How does this also prove your intelligence?

How does believing in your own intelligence change the way you approach tasks?

CHAPTER 41

Limiting Belief #14: I'm Not Ready To Start

*Story – Mary Mother of Jesus
Luke 1:26-38
³⁴"Mary asked the angel, "But how can this happen? I am a virgin." (New Living Translation)*

Previously, you've worked hard at overcoming limiting beliefs that have the power to stop you. However, what if a belief is keeping you from getting started in the first place? Discover how to get moving in this chapter.

You have something big and exciting that you want to do…but you don't feel like you're ready to launch. You don't feel like you have enough of the pieces in place in order to effectively get started. And so, you wait. And wait. And wait.

You keep trying to get everything just perfect so that you can get started.

However, with this mentality, you'll never actually get started. If you wait until everything is perfect in order to launch, you'll never launch. Because nothing will ever actually be perfect. You'll never get every single duck in a row. You'll never be fully ready to start.

The reality is that, eventually, you just need to get going anyway.

Your limiting belief is that you're not ready to start until everything is perfect.

This limiting belief keeps you from achieving the great things you could achieve. Instead of getting started and then adjusting as necessary, you never get started at all. Your ideas never make it out of the idea stage. You don't take action.

Rewriting The Limiting Belief

Now let's rewrite this limiting belief with a set of empowering beliefs.

Limiting Belief:

- "I'm not ready to start."

Empowering Belief:

- "Progress matters more than perfection."
- "I can always make changes as I go."
- "If I wait until everything is perfect, I'll never get started."
- "I should start sooner rather than later."
- "I can't wait around for my dreams to come true."

You must understand that what truly matters is progress, not perfection. Getting started matters more than getting everything perfect. There comes a time when you simply must hit the "Go" button.

Once you get started, you can make the necessary corrections. You can adjust your course as needed. But if you wait until you feel perfectly ready to launch, you will never launch at all. If you wait until everything is just so, your dreams will die before they ever see the light of day.

Your new belief is that you'll get started now and make changes as necessary.

It's better to start and to make mistakes than to never get started. You can always fix things along the way. You can always make changes when the time comes.

You absolutely must not wait until the time is "perfect" because there will never be a perfect time to get started.

Action Steps

- Make a list of the *minimum* number of things necessary for you to do in order to launch your idea.
- Each day, work on one of those things.
- Once you've completed the list, launch your idea into the world.
- Make corrections as necessary as time goes on.

Affirmation

I believe in getting started now. I avoid waiting until all things are perfect in order to get started with my idea. I do my best to get things in order, but I refuse to believe the lie that everything can be perfect. I know that nothing can be perfect.

So, instead of waiting, I take action.

I get started and then make corrections as necessary. Fear and perfectionism lack the power to hold me back.

I move forward with confidence to achieve my dreams and create the life I desire.

Looking Forward

Yay! By overcoming this self-limiting belief, you're now ready to launch yourself toward your big goals! Please join us in the last chapter—self-limiting belief a summary and reflection to solidify your new beliefs before you go.

Self-Reflection Questions

Why is it so easy to put off starting a task or project?

How does trying to get everything perfect actually keep you from achieving your dreams?

Is there ever a "perfect" time to launch a project or task?

When is the best time to get started?

CHAPTER 42

Summary - No More Limits! Overcoming Your Self-Limiting Beliefs

Practical Application

Faith

Self-Limiting beliefs are beliefs that you hold consciously or subconsciously that keep you from achieving your goals and creating the good life you deserve.

You discovered many common limiting beliefs that may be stopping you - keeping you stuck in routines of frustration, worry, and despair. You learned techniques to conquer these negative beliefs and instill new, positive beliefs in their place.

Fitness

This is not one-and-done kind of work but a marathon, day-by-day kind of work. Mentally, emotionally, heart-filled, and financially fit work to tackle these self-limiting beliefs.

The limiting beliefs that you discovered how to overcome are:

1. I don't have enough time.
2. I'm too old to start something new.
3. Past failure means future failure.
4. My past will always negatively influence my future.
5. My resources are limited.
6. Lack of major progress means failure.
7. I compare myself to others.
8. I am not responsible for my current situation.
9. I don't deserve success.
10. I worry about what others think about me.
11. I don't give myself the love, compassion, and understanding I give to others.
12. I can do everything myself.
13. I'm not smart enough.
14. I'm not ready to start.

Finances

Tackling some of the above will undoubtably require an investment of time. Time is money.

For example, you are already smart enough. You purchased this book. But you may want to increase your intelligence. That may involve investing in more books. Attending conferences and seminars.

How about investing in an Executive Coach like myself?

Family and Friends

Learning how to transform these beliefs can help you to discover and work on other limiting beliefs that you may have. Simply apply the same strategies that you've learned here to any other limiting beliefs that you find stopping you.

For best results, focus on changing only one or two at a time. Don't hesitate to solicit the help of family or friends in your quest. Accountability partners are good to check in with as to your progress. Not for them to weigh-in necessarily. Moreso, for you to set deadlines and have someone to support you in successfully meeting those deadlines.

Festivities

Celebrate your wins by answering the self-reflections questions openly and honestly.

Celebrate your newfound freedom by being unabashedly transparent with yourself.

After you've answered a few questions, take a break. Go for a long walk. Do something you enjoy. Hey, enjoy a guilty pleasure; ice cream, a trip to the mall to window shop...etc.

Self-Reflection Questions and Activities

Use these questions to reflect on what you've learned and empower yourself to go after your goals.

- How are limiting beliefs affecting your life?
- Which limiting beliefs have the most negative impact on you?

- Can you think of additional beliefs that may be stopping you? For each one, write a new, empowering belief that you can replace it with.
- Choose one limiting belief to focus on changing immediately and take action today to start replacing it with your new, empowering belief. Affirm this new belief in writing with an affirmation. Keep your affirmation where you can see it. Repeat your new affirmation throughout each day.

Go Forth and Conquer

You now know how to overcome some of the most powerful limiting beliefs that hold you back. You have a firm strategy in place for identifying them and then replacing the limiting beliefs with empowering beliefs.

Most people are unaware of these limiting beliefs. But not you. You will no longer be held captive by them. You will no longer let them keep you from reaching your full potential. You have been given the truth, and the truth will set you free.

So, start crushing your self-limiting beliefs today. Don't let them hold you back any longer. Don't put up with them. Limiting beliefs truly do limit you. They keep you from being the person you were meant to be. They keep you from accomplishing all the glorious love and money goals you could accomplish.

Conquer your limiting beliefs today! You'll be so glad you did!

Prayer

God thank you for the reveal. Revealing and exposing the

self-limiting beliefs that have held me back for experiencing life to the fullest. Thank You for healing. Healing the hurts that caused the seeds of doubt to be planted in my heart. Releasing me from past disappointments and failures. Thank You for sealing the deal and keeping your promises as I trust You and the process. Thank you for helping me CRUSH these beliefs and REPLACE them with more positive, affirming ones. Let it be so, and so it is.

Promise

_____
_____
_____
_____
_____
_____
_____
_____
_____
_____
_____
_____
_____
_____
_____
_____
_____
_____
_____
_____
_____
_____

CHAPTER 43

Aha Moments

"I had only heard about you before, but now I have seen you with my own eyes". Job 42:5 (New Living Translation)

That is my FAVORITE verse of scripture in the Bible. Every time I read it, my heart races and tears form in my eyes.

My emotions stem from a grateful heart that my grandmothers and my parents introduced me to God BUT, when I got to know God for myself my entire life changed. Getting to know God personally, even at the tender age of five, was my aha moment.

Every time, I had to be reminded of my relationship with God and God's love for me, has been my aha moment.

As an avid reader, when I read a book full of nuggets, I always jot down my aha moments. Well, since I'm writing this book, full of golden nuggets, I thought I'd add a section just for your aha moments.

Go for it!

CHAPTER 44

Transparency – My Why

Because I always want to know what inspired an author to write the book they've written, I thought it would be cool to include my 'why'.

I have been an avid, ferocious reader of self-help, biographies, motivational, inspiration, how-to, religious, romance, and mystery books since elementary school.

However, when I've read the most of those genres, I've had to look at them through lens or filter of being a single mother.

Climbing the corporate ladder, while raising two children was a challenge. I read books and took classes to learn how to do them both, but I had to modify accordingly for my circumstance or situation.

I thought about how nice it would've been to have at my fingertips a how to guide, motivational, self-help, inspirational book that had me in mind.

I'm writing the book after the fact.

My children are amazing young adults that are contributing members in society. I have a career I absolutely love. I live in an area where there are far more sunny days than rainy ones. I have an online business that is flourishing and quickly replacing my day job.

God is amazing. Life is good and full of love. Economic liberation is possible and sweet.

This is my offering to single mothers, globally.

ABOUT THE AUTHOR

The Belief System (B.S.) Boss®, Dr. Lisa T. Lewis, helps career-minded single mothers provide abundantly for their families and still achieve their love and money goals, guilt, and stress-free through her "B.S." (Belief System) training. A certified John Maxwell Team Coach. TEDx Talk-International Speaker. Clergy. Writer. Dr. Lisa is also the best-selling author of Making B.S. Boss Moves: The Four R's to Achieve Success, The B.S. Boss Blueprint: A Guide to Perpetually Succeed, and Single Moms Guide to Love and Money: Five Keys to Unlock Both.

- 31+ Years of Leadership & Management in the Public Sector (Budget and Finance)
- Certificate in Public Leadership (The Brookings Institute)
- Certificate in Personal Development & Executive Coaching (The Coaching and Positive Psychology Institute)
- Ordained Elder/Clergy (Greater Saint John Cathedral)
- The President's Lifetime Achievement Award 2018
- Humanitarian Award 2018 (Trinity International University of Ambassadors, Atlanta, GA)
- Honorary Doctor of Divinity (Trinity International University of Ambassadors, Atlanta, GA)

She is available to do podcasts, interviews, facilitate workshops, and give Key Notes. She may be reached by phone at 833-542-2697, email info@DrLisaTLewis.com or social media:

Visit here at https://linktr.ee/iamdrlisatlewis

www.ingramcontent.com/pod-product-compliance
Lightning Source LLC
Chambersburg PA
CBHW071234070526
44583CB00017B/2176